Contents

iii

Privilege,
Power,
and Difference

Second Edition

Allan G. Johnson, Ph.D.

Boston   Burr Ridge, IL   Dubuque, IA   Madison, WI   New York
San Francisco   St. Louis   Bangkok   Bogotá   Caracas   Kuala Lumpur
Lisbon   London   Madrid   Mexico City   Milan   Montreal   New Delhi
Santiago   Seoul   Singapore   Sydney   Taipei   Toronto

The *McGraw-Hill* Companies

Mc Graw Hill **Higher Education**

Published by McGraw-Hill, an imprint of The McGraw-Hill Companies, Inc.
1221 Avenue of the Americas, New York, NY 10020. Copyright © 2006, 2001
by The McGraw-Hill Companies, Inc. All rights reserved. No part of this
publication may be reproduced or distributed in any form or by any means,
or stored in a database or retrieval system, without the prior written consent
of The McGraw-Hill Companies, Inc., including, but not limited to, in any
network or other electronic storage or transmission, or broadcast for distance
learning. Some ancillaries, including electronic and print components, may
not be available to customers outside the United States.

1 2 3 4 5 6 7 8 9 0 DOC/DOC 0 9 8 7 6 5
ISBN 0-07-287489-9

Allan Johnson is a frequent speaker on college and university campuses.
If you would like to arrange an event, you can reach him by e-mail at
agjohnson@mail.hartford.edu. For more on his work, visit his Web site at
www.agjohnson.us.

Vice president and editor-in-chief, Emily Barrosse; publisher, Philip A.
Butcher; sponsoring editor, Sherith Pankratz; media producer, Jessica Bodie;
production editor, Mel Valentin; design manager, Preston Thomas; art editor,
Emma Ghiselli; production supervisor, Tandra Jorgensen. The text was set in
10.5/14 New Baskerville by GTS-India and printed on acid-free, Windsor
Offset Smooth by RR Donnelly, Crawfordsville.

Library of Congress Cataloging-in-Publication Data
Johnson, Allan G.
  Privilege, power, and difference/Allan G. Johnson.
    p. cm.
  Includes bibliographical references and index.
  ISBN 0-07-287489-9
  1. Elite (Social sciences)–United States. 2. Power (Social sciences)–United States.
  3. Social conflict–United States. I. Title.

HN90.E4J642005
305.5'0973–dc22   2004064987
www.mhhe.com

Stubborn Ounces: What Can We Do?   136

For Jane Tuohy

Introduction

I wrote this little book for one reason. We all know that a great deal of trouble surrounds issues of privilege, power, and difference in this society, trouble relating to gender and race, sexual orientation, ethnicity, disability status, social class. A huge store of knowledge, from scientific research to passionate memoirs, documents this trouble and leaves no doubt that it causes enormous amounts of injustice and unnecessary suffering.

For all that we know, however, we still don't seem to have an understanding of the trouble we're in that allows us to do something about it. We are, both individually and collectively, stuck in a kind of paralysis that perpetuates the trouble and its human consequences.

All of us are part of the problem. There is no way to avoid that as long as we live in the world. But we can also make ourselves part of the solution if we know how. This book provides a way of thinking about the trouble that can help us become part of the solution by getting us unstuck. It provides a framework that is conceptual and theoretical on the one hand and grounded in the experience of everyday life on the other. Thus it allows us to see not only where the trouble comes from but also how we as individuals are connected to it, which is the only thing that gives us the potential to make a difference.

When most people read the phrase "how we as individuals are connected to it," they think they're about to be told they've done something wrong, that blame and guilt aren't far behind, especially if they are white or male or heterosexual or nondisabled or of a privileged class. This defensive reaction has done more than perhaps anything else to keep us stuck in our current paralysis by preventing each of us from taking the steps required to become part of the solution.

As a white, male, heterosexual, nondisabled, middle-class professional, I know about such feelings from my own life. But as a sociologist, I also know that it's possible to understand the world and myself in relation to it in ways that get past defensive feelings and give us all a common ground from which to work for change. My purpose in this book is to articulate that understanding in ways that are clear and compelling and, above all, useful. The sociological framework the book offers is conceptual and theoretical. It is about how we think. But always the purpose is to change how we think so that we can change how we act and, by changing how we participate in the world, become part of the complex dynamic through which the world itself will change.

Because my primary goal is to change how people think about issues of difference and privilege, I've been less concerned with describing all the forms that privilege can take and the problems associated with them. In choosing, I've been drawn to forms of privilege that are the most pervasive, that affect the greatest number of people, and that produce the most harm. Also, like any author, I tend to stick to what I know best. As a result, I focus almost entirely on gender, race, social class, disability status, and sexual orientation.

Those who are familiar with the first edition of *Privilege, Power, and Difference* will notice that the 2nd edition includes issues of disability, and it's important to say something about how that came about. Why wasn't it included in the first edition? The main reason is that I, as a nondisabled person, was blinded by my own privilege to the reality of how disability status affects people. After the first edition was published, I heard from several readers—most notably Marshall Mitchell, who teaches disability studies at Washington State University—who urged me to reconsider. What followed was a long period during which I had to educate myself and listen to those who knew more about this than I did. In short, I had to come to terms with what I didn't know about privilege and what I thought I *did* know, which is to say, I had to do for myself what I've written this book to help others to do.

Simple ignorance, however, is not the whole story, for the difficulty nondisabled people have in seeing and understanding their privilege and the oppression of people who are socially identified as disabled is rooted in the driving force behind this form of privilege.

Unlike race, gender, and sexual orientation, disability status can change during a person's lifetime. In fact, as the saying goes, everyone will experience some form of disability during their lives unless they die first. People with disabilities, then, are a constant reminder of the full reality of the human experience—how vulnerable we are and how much there is in life that we cannot control. For many nondisabled people, this is a frightening thing to contemplate. Treating people with disabilities as if they were invisible, designing buildings as if everyone was nondisabled, seeing people with disabilities as inferior or abnormal, even less than human—all these aspects of their oppression enable nondisabled people to deny a basic truth of the human condition.

Accepting the human condition is especially difficult for nondisabled people in the United States, where the ideal of being autonomous and independent, needing no one's help to get along, is strongly rooted in the culture. As any student of society and social life knows, however, these are myths, because from the time that we are born to the moment that we die, human beings depend on other human beings for their very existence. But being mythical does not lessen the power of such ideas, and I have had to come to terms with how they have affected my writing of this book.

You might be wondering at this point why I use the word *nondisabled* to refer to people without disabilities. Wouldn't *abled* be a simpler and more direct way to put it? Yes, but it would also cover up the reason for including disability issues in a book on privilege.

Consider this: if I have use of my eyes, and you are blind, it's reasonable to say that I have an ability and you have an inability. Or, put differently, when it comes to using eyes to see, I am "abled," and you are "disabled." I might go on to point out that my condition gives me certain advantages, and I'd be right, although you might counter that your condition gives you access to experiences, insights, and sensitivities that I'd be less likely to have. You might even assert that your way of seeing is just different from mine and that you don't consider yourself "disabled" at all. Still, if we're looking at the specific ability to use the eyes to see, I think most people would agree that "abled" and "disabled" are reasonable ways to describe this particular objective difference between us.

The problem—and this is where privilege comes in—is that being blind brings with it disadvantages that go beyond not being able to see, whereas not being blind brings with it unearned advantages that go beyond the fact of being able to see. This happens, for example, when the inability to see leads to being labeled a "blind person" or a "disabled person" who is perceived and judged to be nothing more than that—a helpless, damaged, inferior human being who deserves to be treated as such. But, being blind doesn't mean that you're stupid or helpless or inferior or unable to hold a decent job or make your own decisions. It just means you can't see. Even so, you might be discriminated against anyway, giving others—people who can see and therefore aren't perceived as "disabled"—an advantage that they didn't earn.

So, the phrase "nondisability privilege" refers to the privilege of *not* being burdened with the stigma and subordinate status that go along with being identified as "disabled." Admittedly, it's an awkward way to put it, but as is so often the case, systems of privilege don't provide a language that makes it easy to name what's going on.

Readers may also notice that I don't include social class as an example of "privilege, power, and *difference*." I made this choice not from a belief that class is unimportant in people's lives but because the nature and dynamics of class are beyond the scope of what I'm trying to do. My focus is on how differences that would otherwise have little if any inherent connection to social inequality are nonetheless seized on and turned into a basis for privilege and oppression.

Race is perhaps the most obvious example of this. Biologists have long agreed that what are identified as racial differences—skin color being the most prominent—do not define actual biological groups but instead are socially defined categories. More important is that for most of human history, such "differences" have been regarded as socially irrelevant. When white Europeans began to exploit people of color for territorial conquest and economic gain, however, they developed the idea of race as a way to justify their behavior on the grounds of supposed racial superiority. In other words, by itself, something like skin color has no importance at all in social life but was turned into something significant in order to create, justify, and enforce privilege.

Social class, of course, has huge effects on people's lives, but it is not an example of this phenomenon. On the contrary, social class differences are inherently and entirely about privilege. It is also true, however, that class plays an important role in the forms of privilege and oppression that are the focus of this book, which is why I devote an entire chapter (3) to the connection between capitalism on the one hand and privilege, power, and difference on the other. Although racism is a problem that involves all white people, for example, how it plays out in white people's lives varies depending on their social class. For upper-class whites, white privilege may take the form of being able to hire women of color as maids and nannies to do domestic service work they would rather not do themselves or, on a larger scale, to benefit from investments in industries that make use of people of color as a source of cheap labor. In contrast, in the working class, white privilege is more likely to take the form of preferential treatment in hiring and promotion in skilled trades and other upper-level blue-collar occupations, or access to unions or government-subsidized mortgages. Without taking such patterns into account, it's difficult to know just what something like "white privilege" means.

To some degree, this book cannot help having a white, straight, male, nondisabled middle-class point of view, because that's what my background is. But that combination of social characteristics does not simply limit me, for each also provides a bridge from my own experience to some portion of almost every reader's life. I cannot know from my own experience, for example, what it's like to be female or of color or gay in this society. But I can bring my experience as a white person to the struggle of white people—including white women and lower-class white men—to deal with the subject of racism, just as I can bring my experience as a man to men's work—including gay men and men of color—around the subject of sexism and male privilege. In the same way, I can bring my experience as a straight person to the challenge faced by heterosexuals—of whatever gender or race or class—who want to come to terms with heterosexism and homophobia. And I can use my experience of nondisabled privilege to help nondisabled people deal with nondisabled privilege.

What I don't know from my own experience I have to supplement by studying the experience and research and writings of others, which

I've been working at since I received my Ph.D. in sociology more than thirty years ago. During that time, I've designed and taught courses on class and capitalism, the sociology of gender, feminist theory, and, with a female African American colleague, race in the United States. I've written a book on gender inequality (*The Gender Knot: Unraveling Our Patriarchal Legacy*). I've been active in the movement against violence against women and have given presentations to a wide variety of organizations across the United States.

None of this means I'm in a position to say the last word on anything or that this book reflects everyone's experience of difference and privilege. If, however, I've succeeded in what I set out to do here—and only you will know if I have—then I believe the result is a book that has something to offer almost everyone who wants to deal with these difficult issues and help change the world for the better.

Allan G. Johnson
Collinsville, Connecticut
www.agjohnson.us

CHAPTER 1

Rodney King's Question

In 1991, a black motorist named Rodney King suffered a brutal beating at the hands of police officers in Los Angeles. When his assailants were acquitted—in spite of evidence that included a videotape of the incident—and riots broke out in Los Angeles, King uttered the exasperated plea that would become famous as it echoed across the long history and deep divide of racism in the United States. "Can't we all just get along?"

His words formed a simple yet eloquent summary of the current state of our racial dilemma, what the black leader and scholar W. E. B. Du Bois called a century ago "the problem of the color line." But in King's few words, he said more than that. Past his exasperation lies a real and serious question, one that has haunted us ever since the Civil War brought down the institution of U.S. slavery. Like any serious question, it sits and waits for what it deserves, which is a serious answer.

In the 21st century, it is clear that however much people might wish it otherwise, the answer is still no. Whether it's a matter of can't or won't, the truth is that we simply don't get along. Segregation in housing and schools is stubborn and pervasive, and the average wealth of white families is almost 14 times that of blacks. The steady corrosion that everyday racism causes to the fabric of social life is everywhere. It

1

especially galls middle-class blacks who believed what whites told them, that if they did everything right—if they went to school and worked hard and made something of themselves—race would no longer be an issue. But they soon discovered, and they learn anew every day, that nothing seems to protect them from their vulnerability to white racism.[1]

As I write this, I'm aware that some readers—whites in particular, and especially those who don't have the luxury of class privilege—may already feel put off by my use of words like *racism, white,* and, even worse, *white racism.* One way to avoid such reactions is to follow the advice I was once given to not use such words at all. As the rest of this book will make clear, however, if we dispense with the words, we make it impossible to talk about what's really going on and what it has to do with us. And if we can't do that, then we can't see what the problems are or how we might make ourselves part of the solution to them, which is, after all, the only worthwhile point of writing or reading a book such as this.

With that in mind, perhaps the most important thing I can say to reassure readers who are wondering whether to continue is that things are not what they seem. The defensive and irritable feelings that whites often experience when they come across such language are based on fundamental misperceptions of the world, which this book will try to clarify and set straight. If I succeed at that, then the meaning and emotional weight of concepts like "privilege" and "white racism" will soften and shift.

Problems of perception and defensiveness apply not only to the language of race but also to an entire set of social differences that have become the basis for a great deal of trouble in the world. Although Du Bois was correct that color would be a defining issue in the 20th century, the problem of "getting along" doesn't stop there. It is also an issue across differences of gender, sexual orientation, disability status, and numerous lesser divides. Men's violence and harassment aimed at women is epidemic in the United States, for example, and shows no sign of letting up anytime soon. The glass ceiling that lets women see the executive suite but keeps them from being promoted to it is as thick as ever, and the gender gap in income is narrowing only at a glacial pace and persists even among top executives in Fortune 500 companies. Men dominate virtually every major organization and institution, from corporations to government to organized sport and religion, and for all the hype about the "new father," men rarely feel as responsible for domestic work and child care as their female partners do. Harassment and discrimination directed at gay men and lesbians are commonplace, and the threat of physical violence is an ever-present reminder of the dangers of being identified as anything other than heterosexual.

The estimated 54 million people with disabilities in the United States are vulnerable to abuse both within and outside their homes. They are routinely stereotyped as damaged, helpless, and inferior human beings who lack intelligence and are therefore denied the opportunity to develop their abilities fully. The physical environment—from appropriate signage to entrances to buildings, to buses, and airplanes—is designed in ways that make it difficult if not impossible for them to have the information they need and to get from one place to another. Because of such conditions, they are far less likely to finish high school or college and are far more likely to be unemployed and, when they do find work, to be paid less than the minimum wage. The result is a pervasive pattern of exploitation, deprivation, poverty, mistreatment, and isolation that denies access to employment, housing, transportation, information, and basic services needed to fully participate in the life of their society.

Clearly, we aren't getting along with one another, and we need to ask why not.

For many, the answer is some variation on "human nature." People can't help fearing the unfamiliar—including people of other races, goes one popular argument. Or women and men are so dissimilar it's as though they come from separate planets, and it's some kind of cross-cultural (if not cross-species) miracle that we get along as well as we do. Or there is only one natural sexual orientation (heterosexual), and all the rest are therefore unacceptable and bound to cause conflict wherever they become obvious. Or those who are more capable will get more than everyone else—they always have and they always will. Someone, after all, has to be on top.

As popular and powerful as such arguments are, the only way to hold on to them is to ignore most of what history, psychology, anthropology, sociology, biology, and, if people look closely, their own experience reveal about human beings and how they live. We are not prisoners to some natural order that pits us hopelessly and endlessly against one another. We are prisoners to *something*, but it's closer to our own making than we realize.

WE'RE IN TROUBLE

Every morning before breakfast I walk with our dogs, Sophie and Elsie, in acres of woods behind our house in the northwest hills of Connecticut. It's a quiet and peaceful place. I can feel the seasons come and go. Winter lies long and deep beneath one snowfall layered on another. Come spring, fiddlehead ferns uncoil from the forest floor and then summer exhausts itself before sliding into the cool, crisp clarity of autumn.

I like the walks mostly for the solitude. I can reflect on my life and the world and see things in perspective and more clearly. And I like to watch the dogs crash through the woods as they chase each other in games of tag, sniff out fresh deer scat or the trail of an animal that passed through the night before. They go out far and then come back to make sure I'm still there.

It's hard not to notice that everything seems pretty simple to them—or at least from what I can see. They never stray far from what I imagine to be their essence, the core of what it means to be a dog in relation to everything around them, living and otherwise. And that's all they seem to need or care about.

It's also hard not to wonder about my own species, which, by comparison, is deeply troubled most of the time. I suspect we don't have to be, because even though I'm trained as a sociologist to see the complexity of things, it seems to me that we're also fairly simple. Deep in our bones, for example, we are social beings. There's no escaping it. We can't survive on our own when we're young, and it doesn't get a whole lot easier later on. We need to feel that we belong to something bigger than ourselves, whether it's a family or a team or a society. We look to other people to tell us that we measure up, that we matter, that we're okay. We have a huge capacity to be creative and generous and loving. We spin stories, make art and music, help children turn into adults, save one another in countless ways, and ease our loved ones into death when the time comes. We have large brains and opposable thumbs and are incredibly clever in how we use them. I'm not sure if we're the only species with a sense of humor—I think I've known dogs to laugh—but we've certainly made the most of it. And we're astonishingly adaptable. We can figure out how to live just about anywhere under almost any conditions you could imagine. We can take in the strange and unfamiliar and learn to understand and embrace it, whether it's a new language or an odd food or the mysteries of death and dying or the person sitting next to us on the crosstown bus who doesn't look like anyone we've ever seen before.

For all our potential, you'd think we could manage to get along with one another. By that I don't mean love one another in some idealistic way. We don't need to love one another—or even *like* one another—to work together or just share space in the world. I also don't mean something as minimal as mere tolerance or refraining from overt violence. I mean that you'd think we could treat one another with decency and respect and appreciate if not support the best we have in us. It's what I imagine Rodney King meant by "get along."

It doesn't seem unreasonable to imagine a school or a workplace, for example, where all kinds of people feel comfortable showing up, secure in the knowledge that they have a place they don't have to defend every time they turn around, where they're encouraged to do their best, and valued for it. We all like to feel that way—accepted, valued, supported, appreciated, respected, belonging. So you'd think we'd go after it like dogs on the scent of something good to eat. We would, that is, unless something powerful kept us from it.

Apparently, something powerful does keep us from it, to judge from all the trouble there is around issues of difference—especially in relation to race, gender, sexual orientation, disability status, and class. Something powerful keeps us far from anything like a world where people feel comfortable showing up and feel good about themselves and one another. The truth of this powerful force is everywhere, but we don't know how to talk about it, and so we act as though it's always somewhere other than here and not in the room with us.

Several years ago I was sitting across a restaurant table from an African American woman. We were talking about a course on race and gender that we wanted to teach together. And while we talked about what we wanted our students to think about and learn, I felt how hard it was for me to talk about race and gender in that moment—about how the legacy of racism and sexism shapes our lives in such different ways, how my whiteness and maleness are sources of privilege (another of those words that can get people going) that elevates people like me not above some abstract groups, but above people like her, my friend.

The simple truth is that when I go shopping, I'll probably get waited on faster and better than she will. I'll benefit from the cultural assumption that I'm a serious customer who doesn't need to be followed around to keep me from stealing something. The clerk won't ask me for three kinds of ID before accepting my check or accepting my credit card. But all these indignities that my whiteness protects me from are part of her everyday existence. And it doesn't matter how she dresses or behaves or that she's an executive in a large corporation. Her being black and the realtors' and bankers' and clerks' being white in a racist society is all it takes.[2]

She also can't go for a walk alone at night without thinking about her safety a lot more than I would—without planning what to do in case a man approaches her with something other than good will. She has to worry about what a man might think if she smiles in a friendly way and says hello as they pass on the sidewalk, or what he'll think if she doesn't. She has to decide where to park her car for the greatest safety, to remember to have her keys out and ready as she approaches it, and to check the back seat before she gets in. In other words, she has to limit her life in ways that never occur to me, and her being female is the only reason why.[3]

As these thoughts filled my mind, I struggled with how to sit across from her and talk and eat our lunch while all of this is going on all the time. I wanted to say, "Can we talk about this and *us?*" But I didn't, because it felt too risky, the kind of thing both of you know but keep at bay by not actually *saying* it, like a married couple where one's been unfaithful and both know it but collude in silence to keep the thing going. They realize that if either speaks the truth they both already know, they won't be able to go on as if this gulf and hurt between them weren't there.

It's not that I've *done* something or thought bad thoughts or harbored ill will toward her because she's black and female. No, the problem is that in the world as it is, huge issues involving race and gender shape her life and mine in dramatically different ways. And it's not some random accident that befell her while I escaped. A tornado didn't blow through town and level her house while leaving mine alone. No, her misfortune is connected to my good fortune. The reality of her having to deal with racism and sexism every day is connected to the reality that I *don't*. I didn't have to do anything wrong for this to be true and neither did she. But there it is just the same.

All of that sits in the middle of the table like the proverbial elephant that everyone pretends not to notice.

The "elephant" is a society and its people for whom a decent and productive social life that is true to the best of our essential human selves continues to be elusive. In its place is a powerful kind of trouble that is tenacious, profound, and seems only to get worse. I can't help wondering how much worse it will get.

The trouble we're in privileges some groups at the expense of others. It creates a yawning divide in levels of income, wealth, dignity, safety, health, and quality of life. It promotes fear, suspicion, discrimination, harassment, and violence. It sets people against one another. It builds walls topped with broken glass and barbed wire. It weaves the insidious and corroding effects of oppression into the daily lives of tens of millions of women, men, and children. It has the potential to ruin entire generations and, in the long run, to take just about everyone down with it.

It is a trouble that shows up everywhere and touches every life in one way or another. There is no escape, however thick the denial. It's in families and neighborhoods, in schools and churches, in government and the courts, and especially in colleges and the workplace, where many people have their first true experience with people unlike themselves and what this society makes of such differences.

The hard and simple truth is that the "we" that's in trouble is all of us—not just straight, white, nondisabled, middle- and upper-class males—and it will take all or at least most of us to get us out of it. It's relatively easy, for example, for white people to fall into the safe and comfortable rut of thinking that racism is a problem that belongs to people of color. But such thinking mistakes fantasy for reality. It pretends we can talk about "up" without "down" or that a "you" or a "them" can mean something without a "me" or an "us."

There is no way that a problem of difference can involve just one group of people. The "problem" of race can't be just a problem of being black, Chinese, Sioux, or Mexican. It has to be more than that, because there is no way to separate the "problem" of being, say, black from the "problem" of *not* being white. And there is no way to separate the problem of not being white from *being* white. This means privilege is always a problem for people who don't have it and for people who do, because privilege is *always* in relation to others. Privilege is always at someone else's expense and always exacts a cost. Everything that's done to receive or maintain it—however passive and unconscious—results in suffering and deprivation for someone.

We live in a society that attaches privilege to being white and male and heterosexual and nondisabled regardless of social class. If I don't see how that makes me part of the problem of privilege, I won't see myself as part of the solution. And if people in privileged groups don't include themselves in the solution, the default is to leave it to blacks and women and Asians, Latinos/as, Native Americans, lesbians, gay men, people with disabilities, and the lower and working classes to do it on their own. But these groups can't do it on their own, because although they certainly aren't powerless to affect the conditions of their own lives, they do not have the power to singlehandedly do away with entrenched systems of privilege. If they could do that, there wouldn't be a problem in the first place.

The simple truth is that the trouble we're in can't be solved unless people who have privilege feel obligated to make the problem of privilege *their* problem and to do something about it. For me, it means I have to take the initiative to find out how privilege operates in the world, how it affects people, and what that has to do with me. It means I have to think the unthinkable, speak the unspeakable, break the silence, acknowledge the elephant, and then take my share of responsibility for what comes next. It means I have to *do* something to create the possibility for my African American friend and me to have a conversation about race, gender, and us, rather than leave it to her to take all the risks and do all the work. The fact that it's so easy for me and other people in dominant groups not to do this is the single most powerful barrier to change. Understanding how to change that by bringing dominant groups into the conversation and the solution is the biggest challenge we all face.

My work in this book is to help find a way to meet that challenge. It is to identify tools for understanding what's going on and what it's got to do with us without being swallowed up in a sea of guilt and blame or rushing into denial and angry self-defense. It is to open windows to new ways of thinking about difference and what's been made of it in this society. It is to remove barriers that stand between us and serious, long-term conversation *across* difference and effective action for change that can *make* a difference.

We Can't Talk about It
If We Can't Use the Words

As I suggested in the opening pages, you can't deal with a problem if you don't name it. Once you name it, you can think, talk, and write about it, make sense of it by seeing how it's connected to other things that explain it and point toward solutions. Usually the language needed for this comes from people working to solve the problem, especially people most damaged by it. Words like *privilege, racism, sexism, anti-Semitism, heterosexism, classism, ableism, dominance, subordination, oppression,* and *patriarchy* are part of their everyday vocabulary.

When you name something, the word draws your attention to it, which makes you more likely to notice it as something significant. That's why most people have an immediate negative reaction to words like *racism, sexism,* or *privilege.* They don't want to look at what the words point to. Whites don't want to look at racism, nor men at sexism, nor heterosexuals at heterosexism, especially if they have worked hard to improve their class position. People don't want to look because they don't want to know what it has to do with them and how doing something about it might change not only the world but themselves.

So one way to ignore the trouble is to get rid of the words that name it by discrediting them or twisting their meaning or turning them into a phobia or making them invisible. That's what's happened with most words that name the trouble around privilege. It's become almost impossible, for example, to say *sexism* or *male privilege* without most men becoming so uncomfortable and defensive that conversation can't happen. They often act as though *sexism* names a personality flaw found among men, and just saying the word ("Can we talk about sexism today?") is heard as an accusation of a personal moral failure. The same is true of all the other "isms." Since few people like to see themselves as bad, the words are taboo in "polite" company, including many training programs at corporations and universities. So, instead of talking about the racism and sexism that plague people's lives, people talk about "diversity" and "tolerance" and "appreciating difference." Those are good things to talk about, but they're not the same as the isms and the trouble they're connected to.

More than once, I've been asked to talk about the consequences of social domination, subordination, and oppression without actually saying the words *dominant, subordinate,* or *oppression.* At such times, I feel like a doctor trying to help a patient without ever mentioning the body or naming what's wrong. We can't get anywhere that way—and we haven't been. Our collective house is burning down, and we're tiptoeing around afraid to say "Fire."

The bottom line is that a trouble we can't talk about is a trouble we can't do anything about. Words like *sexism* and *privilege* point to something difficult and painful in our history that continues in everyday life in our society. That means there is no way to talk about it without difficulty and without pain. It is possible, however, to talk about it in ways that make the struggle and the pain worth it. To do that, however, we have to reclaim these lost and discredited words so that we can use them to name and make sense of the truth of what's going on.

Reclaiming the words begins with seeing that they rarely mean what most people think they mean. *Racist* isn't another word for "bad white people," just as *patriarchy* isn't a bit of nasty code for "men." *Oppression* and *dominance* name social realities that we can participate in without being oppressive or dominating *people.* And *feminism* isn't an ideology organized around being lesbian or hating men. But you'd never know it by listening to how these words are used in the mass media, popular culture, and over the dinner table. You'd never know such words could be part of a calm and responsible discussion of how to resolve a problem that belongs to all of us.

I use these difficult words freely in this book because I'm writing about the problems they name. Readers who happen to be white or male or heterosexual or economically comfortable or members of some other privileged category will have an easier time of it if they try to tolerate the discomfort such words evoke. I don't use them as accusations. (If I did, I'd have a hard time looking in the mirror.) I don't intend that anyone take them personally.

As a white, male, nondisabled, middle-class heterosexual, I do know that in some ways these words are about me. There's no way to avoid playing some role in the troubles they name, and that's something I need to look at. But in equally important ways, the words are *not* about me because they name something much larger than me, something I didn't invent or create but that was passed on to me as a legacy when I was born into this society. If I'm going to be part of the solution to that difficult legacy, I must step back from my defensive sensitivity to such language and look at the reality it points to. Then I can understand what it names and what it has to do with me and, most important, what I can do about it.

CHAPTER 2

Privilege, Oppression, and Difference

The trouble that surrounds difference is really about privilege and power—the existence of privilege and the lopsided distribution of power that keeps it going. The trouble is rooted in a legacy we all inherited, and while we're here, it belongs to us. It isn't our fault, but now that it's ours, it's up to us to decide how we're going to deal with it before we pass it along to generations to come.

Talking openly about power and privilege isn't easy, which is why people rarely do. The reason for this seems to be a fear of anything that might make dominant groups uncomfortable or "pit groups against each other,"[1] even though groups are *already* pitted against one another by the structures of privilege that organize society as a whole. The fear keeps us from looking at what's going on and makes it impossible to do anything about the reality that lies deeper down.

DIFFERENCE IS NOT THE PROBLEM

Ignoring privilege keeps us in a state of unreality by promoting the illusion that difference by itself is the problem. In some ways, of course, it can be a problem when people try to work together across cultural divides that set groups up to think and do things their own way. But human beings have been overcoming such divides for thousands of years as a matter of routine. The real illusion connected to difference is the popular assumption that people are naturally afraid of what they don't know or understand. This supposedly makes it inevitable that you'll fear and distrust people who aren't like you and, in spite of your good intentions, you'll find it all but impossible to get along with them.

For all its popularity, the idea that everyone is naturally frightened by difference is a cultural myth that, more than anything, justifies keeping outsiders on the outside and treating them badly if they happen to get in. The mere fact that something is new or strange isn't enough to make us afraid of it. When Europeans first came to North America, for example, they weren't terribly afraid of the people they encountered, and the typical Native American response was to welcome these astonishingly "different" people with open arms (much to their later regret). Scientists, psychotherapists, inventors, novelists (and their fans), explorers, philosophers, spiritualists, anthropologists, and the just plain curious are all drawn toward the mystery of what they don't know. Even children—probably the most vulnerable form that people come in—seem to *love* the unknown, which is why parents are always worrying about what their toddler has gotten into *now.*

There is nothing inherently frightening about what we don't know. If we feel afraid, it isn't what we *don't* know that frightens us, it's what we *think* we *do* know. The problem is our ideas about what we don't know—what might happen next or what's lurking behind that unopened door or in the mind of the "strange"-looking guy sitting across from us on the nearly empty train. And how we think about such things isn't something we're born with. We learn to do it as we learn to tie our shoes, talk, and do just about everything else. If we take difference and diversity as reasons for fear and occasions for trouble, it's because we've learned to think about them in ways that *make* for fear and trouble. Marshall Mitchell, who teaches disability studies at Washington State University, tells of children who "approach me in my wheelchair with no hesitation or fear, but each year that they get older they become more fearful. Why? Because they are then afraid of what they've been taught and think they know."[2]

MAPPING DIFFERENCE: WHO ARE WE?

Issues of difference cover a large territory. A useful way to put it in perspective is with the "diversity wheel" (Figure 1) developed by Marilyn Loden and Judy Rosener.[3] In the hub of the wheel are six social characteristics: age, race, ethnicity, gender, physical ability and qualities (left/right-handedness, height, and so on), and sexual orientation. Around the outer ring are several others, including religion, marital and parental status, and social-class indicators such as education, occupation, and income.

Anyone can describe themselves by going around the wheel. Starting in the hub, I'm male, English-Norwegian (as far as I know), white (also as far as I know), fifty-nine years old, heterosexual, and nondisabled (so far). In the outer ring, I'm married, a father and grandfather, and a middle-class professional with a Ph.D. I've lived in New England for most of my life, but I've also lived in other countries. I have a vaguely Christian background, but if I had to identify my spiritual life with a particular tradition, I'd lean more toward Buddhism than anything else. I served a brief stint in the Army reserves.

It would be useful if you stopped reading for a moment and do what I just did. Go around the diversity wheel and get a sense of yourself in terms of it.

As you reflect on the results of this exercise, it might occur to you (as it did to me) that the wheel doesn't say much about the unique individual you know yourself to be, your personal history, the content of your character, what you dream and feel. It does, however, say a lot about the social reality that shapes everyone's life in powerful ways.

Imagine, for example, that you woke up tomorrow morning and found that your race was different from what it was when you went to bed (the plot of a 1970 movie called *Watermelon Man*). Or imagine that your gender or sexual orientation had changed (as happened to the central character in Virginia Woolf's novel *Orlando*). How would that affect how people perceive you and treat you? How would it affect how you see yourself? How would it change the material circumstances of your life, such as where you live or how much money you have? In what ways would the change make life better? In what ways worse?

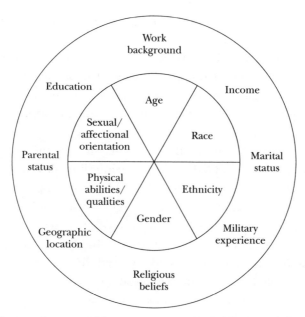

FIGURE 1. The Diversity Wheel. From *Workforce America* by M. Loden and J. Rosener, McGraw-Hill, 1991. Reproduced with permission from the McGraw-Hill Companies.

In answering these questions, try to go beyond the obvious consequences to see the ones that are perhaps more subtle. If you're heterosexual now, for example, and wake up gay or lesbian, your sexual feelings about women and men would be different. But what about how people perceive you and treat you in ways unrelated to sex? Would people treat you differently at school or work? Would friends treat you differently? Parents and siblings? In similar ways, what changes would you experience in switching from female to male or from male to female, from white to African American, from Asian or Latina/o to Anglo, or from nondisabled to using a wheelchair or a white cane? Again, focus on the social consequences, on how people would perceive you and treat you if such a thing happened to you. What opportunities would open or close? What rewards would or wouldn't come your way?

For most people, shifting only a few parts of the diversity wheel would be enough to change their lives dramatically. Even though the characteristics in the wheel may not tell us who we are as individuals in the privacy of our hearts and souls, they matter a great deal because they locate us in relation to other people and society in ways that can have huge consequences.

The trouble around diversity, then, isn't just that people differ from one another. The trouble is produced by a world organized in ways that encourage people to *use* difference to include or exclude, reward or punish, credit or discredit, elevate or oppress, value or devalue, leave alone or harass.

This is especially true of the characteristics in the center of the wheel, which have the added quality of being difficult if not impossible to change (except acquiring a disability, which can happen to anyone at any time). It's true that sex-change surgery is available and that it's possible for some people to "pass" for a race or sexual orientation that is other than what they know themselves to be. But this is quite different from being married one day and divorced the next, or getting a new job that suddenly elevates your class position. Unlike the outer portion of the wheel, the inner portion consists of characteristics that, one way or another, we must learn to live with regardless of how we choose to reveal ourselves to others.

Perceptions are difficult to control, however, because people tend to assume that they can identify characteristics such as race and gender simply by looking at someone. We routinely form quick impressions of race, gender, age, sexual orientation, or disability status. Sometimes these impressions are based on blanket assumptions—that everyone, for example, is heterosexual until proven otherwise. Or if they *look* "white," they *are* white. People usually form such impressions without thinking and rely on them in order to see the world as an organized and predictable place from one moment to the next.

We may not realize how routinely we form such impressions until we run into someone who doesn't fit neatly into one of our categories, especially gender or sexual orientation. Pass someone on the street whom you can't identify as clearly male or female, for example, and it can jolt your attention and nag you until you think you've figured it out.

Our culture allows for only two genders (compared with some cultures that recognize several), and anyone who doesn't clearly fit one or the other is instantly perceived as an outsider. This is why babies born with a mixture of sex characteristics are routinely altered surgically in order to "fit" the culturally defined categories of female and male. In contrast, among the Native American Navaho, a person born with physical characteristics that weren't clearly male or female was placed in a third category—called *nadle*—which was considered just as legitimate as *female* and *male*. In some Native American plains tribes, people were allowed to choose their gender regardless of their physical characteristics, as when men might respond to a spiritual vision by taking on the dress of women.[4]

Most of our ways of thinking about sexuality are also based on social construction. Whether gay or lesbian behavior is regarded as normal or deviant, for example, depends on the cultural context, as does the larger question of whether sexual orientation is perceived as defining the kind of human being you are and the way you live your life.

So the characteristics at the center of the wheel are usually very hard to change, are the object of quick and firm impressions that can profoundly affect our lives. Clearly, diversity isn't just about the "variety" that the word suggests. Diversity *could* just be about that, but only in some other world.[5]

THE SOCIAL CONSTRUCTION
OF DIFFERENCE

The late African American novelist James Baldwin once offered the provocative idea that there is no such thing as whiteness or, for that matter, blackness or, more generally, race. "No one is white before he/she came to America," he wrote. "It took generations, and a vast amount of coercion, before this became a white country."[6]

What did Baldwin mean? In the simplest sense, he was pointing to a basic aspect of social reality: most of what we experience as "real" is a cultural creation. In other words, it's made up, even though we don't experience it that way.

Take race, for example. Baldwin isn't denying the reality that skin pigmentation varies from one person to another. What he is saying is that unless you live in a culture that recognizes such differences as significant, they are socially irrelevant and therefore, in a way, do not exist. A "black woman" in Africa, therefore, who has not experienced white racism, does not *think* of herself as black or experience herself as black, nor do the people around her. African, yes, a woman, yes. But not a *black* woman.

When she comes to the United States, however, where privilege is organized according to race, suddenly she becomes black because people assign her to a social category that bears that name, and they treat her differently as a result. In similar ways, as Baldwin argues, a Norwegian farmer has no reason to think of himself as white so long as he's in Norway. But when he comes to the United States, one of the first things he discovers is the significance of being considered white and the privilege that goes along with it. And so he is eager to adopt "white" as part of his identity and to make sure that others acknowledge it.

So Baldwin is telling us that race and all its categories have no significance outside systems of privilege and oppression in which they were created in the first place.[7] This is what sociologists call the "social construction" of reality.

One way to see the constructed nature of reality is to notice how the definitions of different "races" change historically, by including groups at one time that were excluded in another. The Irish, for example, were long considered by the dominant white Anglo-Saxon Protestants of England and the United States to be members of a nonwhite "race," as were Italians, Jews, Greeks, and people from a number of Eastern European countries. As such, immigrants from these groups to England and the United States were excluded and subjugated and exploited in much the same way that blacks were. This was especially true of the Irish in Ireland in relation to the British, who for centuries treated them as an inferior race. Note, however, that their skin color was indistinguishable from that of those considered to be "white." If anything, the skin of most people of Irish descent is "fairer" than that of others of European heritage. But their actual complexion didn't matter, because the dominant racial group has the cultural authority to define the boundaries around "white" as it chooses.

The same is true with the definition of what is considered "normal." While it may come as a surprise to many who think of themselves as nondisabled, disability and nondisability are socially constructed. This doesn't mean that the difference between having or not having full use of your legs is somehow "made up" without any objective reality. It does mean, however, that how people notice and label and think about such differences and how they treat other people as a result depend entirely on ideas contained in a system's culture.

Human beings, for example, come in a variety of heights, and many of those considered "normal" are unable to reach high places such as kitchen shelves without the assistance of physical aids—chairs and step-stools. In spite of their inability to do this simple task without special aids, they are not defined as disabled. Nor are the roughly 100 million people in the United States who cannot see properly without the aid of eyeglasses. Why? Because the dominant group—like all dominant groups—has the power to define what is considered normal. In contrast, people who use wheelchairs, for example, to get from one place to another—to "reach" places they cannot otherwise go— do not have the social power to define their condition as within the boundaries of normality, that is, as little more than a manifestation of the simple fact that in the normal course of life, people come in a wide variety of shapes and sizes and physical and mental conditions.

Disability and nondisability are also constructed through the language used to describe people. When someone who cannot see is labeled a "blind person," for example, it creates the impression that not being able to see sums up the entire person. In other words, blind becomes what they *are*. The same thing happens when people are described as "brain damaged" or "crippled" or "retarded" or "deaf"— the person becomes the disability and nothing more. Reducing people to a single dimension of who they are separates and excludes them, marks them as "other," as different from "normal" (white, heterosexual, male, nondisabled) people and therefore as inferior. The effect is compounded by portraying people with disabilities as helpless victims who are "confined" or "stricken" or "suffering from" some "affliction" and then lumping them into an undifferentiated class—*the* blind, *the* crippled, *the* retarded, *the* deaf, *the* disabled.

Of course, using a wheelchair or being unable to see or hear affects people's lives, and pointing out that disability and nondisability are socially constructed is not intended to imply otherwise. But there is a world of difference between using a wheelchair and being treated as a normal human being (who happens to use a wheelchair to get around) and using a wheelchair and being treated as invisible, inferior, unintelligent, asexual, frightening, passive, dependent, and nothing more than your disability. And that difference is not a matter of the disability itself but of how it is constructed in society and how we then make use of that construction in our minds to shape how we think about ourselves and other people and how we treat them as a result.

What makes socially constructed reality so powerful is that we rarely if ever experience it as that. We think the way our culture defines something like race or gender is simply the way things are in some objective sense. We think there really is such a thing as "race" and that the words we use simply name an objective reality that is "out there." The truth is, however, that once human beings give something a name—whether it be skin color or disability—that thing acquires a significance it otherwise would not have. More important, the name quickly takes on a life of its own as we forget the social process that created it and start treating it as "real" in and of itself.

This process is what allows us to believe that something like "race" actually points to a set of clear and unambiguous categories into which people fall, ignoring the fact that the definition of various races changes all the time and is riddled with inconsistencies and overlapping boundaries. In the 19th century, for example, U.S. law identified those having *any* African ancestry as black, a standard known as the "one-drop rule," which defined "white" as a state of absolute purity in relation to "black." Native American status, in contrast, required at *least* one-eighth Native American ancestry in order to qualify. Why the different standards? Adrian Piper argues that it was mostly a matter of economics. Native Americans could claim financial benefits from the federal government, making it to whites' advantage to make it hard for anyone to be considered Native American. Designating someone as black, however, took *away* power and *denied* the right to make claims against whites, including white families of origin. In both cases, racial classification has had little to do with objective characteristics and everything to do with preserving white power and wealth.[8]

This fact has also been true of the use of race to tag various ethnic groups. When the Chinese were imported as cheap laborers during the 19th century, the California Supreme Court declared them not white. Mexicans, however, many of whom owned large amounts of land in California and did business with whites, were considered white.

Today, as Paul Kivel points out, Mexicans are no longer considered white and the Chinese are "conditionally white at times."[9]

When the stakes are privilege and power, dominant groups are quite willing to ignore such inconsistencies so long as the result is a continuation of their privilege.

WHAT IS PRIVILEGE?

No matter what privileged group you belong to, if you want to understand the problem of privilege and difference, the first stumbling block is usually the idea of privilege itself. When people hear that they belong to a privileged group or benefit from something like "white privilege" or "male privilege," they don't get it, or they feel angry and defensive about what they do get. *Privilege* has become one of those loaded words we need to reclaim so that we can use it to name and illuminate the truth. Denying that privilege exists is a serious barrier to change, so serious that it is the subject of a whole chapter (Chapter 7). But it's important to get a sense of what the word means before we go any further.

As Peggy McIntosh describes it, privilege exists when one group has something of value that is denied to others simply because of the groups they belong to, rather than because of anything they've done or failed to do.[10] If people take me more seriously when I give a speech than they would someone of color saying the same things in the same way, then I'm benefiting from white privilege. That a heterosexual black woman can feel free to talk about her life in ways that reveal the fact that she's married to a man is a form of heterosexual privilege because lesbians and gay men cannot casually reveal their sexual orientation without putting themselves at risk.

Notice that in all these examples, it's relatively easy for people to be unaware of how privilege affects them. When people come up to me after I give a presentation, for example, it doesn't occur to me that they'd probably be more critical and less positive if I were Latino or female or gay. I don't *feel* privileged in that moment. I just feel that I did a good job, and I enjoy the rewards that are supposed to go with it.

The existence of privilege doesn't mean I *didn't* do a good job or that I don't deserve credit for it. What it does mean is that I'm *also* getting something that other people are denied, people who are like me in every respect except for the social categories they belong to. In this sense, my access to privilege doesn't determine my outcomes, but it is definitely an *asset* that makes it more likely that whatever talent, ability, and aspirations I have will result in something good for me.[11] In the same way, being female or of color doesn't determine people's outcomes, but these characteristics are turned into *liabilities* that make it less likely that people's talent, ability, and aspirations will be recognized and rewarded.

This is also true of people with disabilities. Nondisabled people often assume that people with disabilities lack intelligence and are little more than needy, helpless victims who can't take care of themselves and whose achievements and situation in life depend solely on their physical or mental condition and not on how they are treated or the physical or attitudinal obstacles that are placed in their way.[12]

The ease of not being aware of privilege is an aspect of privilege itself, what some call "the luxury of obliviousness" (or, in philosophy, "epistemic privilege"). Awareness requires effort and commitment. Being able to command the attention of lower-status individuals without having to give it in return is a key aspect of privilege. African Americans, for example, have to pay close attention to whites and white culture and get to know them well enough to avoid displeasing them, since whites control jobs, schools, government, the police, and most other resources and sources of power. White privilege gives whites little reason to pay attention to African Americans or to how white privilege affects them. In other words, as James Baldwin put it, "To be white in America means not having to think about it."[13] We could say the same thing about maleness or any other basis for privilege. So strong is the sense of entitlement behind this luxury that males, whites, and others can feel put upon in the face of even the mildest invitation to pay attention to issues of privilege. "We shouldn't *have* to look at this stuff," they seem to say. "It isn't *fair.*"

TWO TYPES OF PRIVILEGE

According to McIntosh, privilege comes in two types. The first is based on what she calls "unearned entitlements," which are things of value that all people *should* have, such as feeling safe in public spaces or working in a place where they feel they belong and are valued for what they can contribute. When an unearned entitlement is restricted to certain groups, however, it becomes a form of privilege she calls "unearned advantage."

In some cases, it's possible to do away with unearned advantages without anyone losing out. If the workplace changed so that *everyone* was valued for what they could contribute, for example, that privilege would disappear without the dominant group having to give up their own sense that *they* are valued for their contributions. The unearned entitlement would then be available to all and, as such, would no longer be a form of unearned advantage.

In many other cases, however, unearned advantage gives dominant groups a competitive edge they are reluctant to even acknowledge, much less give up. This is particularly true of lower-, working-, and lower-middle-class whites and males who know all too well the price they pay for a lack of class privilege and how hard it is to improve their lives and hang on to what they've managed to achieve. Their lack of class privilege, however, can blind them to the fact that the cultural valuing of whiteness and maleness over color and femaleness gives them an edge in most situations that involve evaluations of credibility or competence. To give up that advantage would double or even triple the amount of competition. This would especially affect white males, who are a shrinking numerical minority of the U.S. population. A loss of race and gender privilege would level the playing field to admit white women and people of color, a combined group that outnumbers white males by a large margin.

The second form of privilege—what McIntosh calls "conferred dominance"—goes a step further by giving one group power over another. The common pattern of men controlling conversations with women, for example, is grounded in a cultural assumption that men are supposed to dominate women. An adolescent boy who appears too willing to defer to his mother risks being called a "mama's boy," in the same way that a husband who appears in any way subordinate to his wife is often labeled "henpecked" (or worse). The counterpart for girls carries no such stigma. "Daddy's girl" isn't considered an insult in this culture, and the language contains *no* specific insulting terms for a wife who is under the control of her husband.

Conferred dominance also manifests itself in race privilege. In his book *The Rage of a Privileged Class,* for example, the African American journalist Ellis Cose tells the story of an African American lawyer, a partner in a large firm, who goes to the office early one Saturday morning to catch up on some work and is confronted near the elevator by a recently hired young white attorney.

"Can I help you?" the white man says pointedly.

The partner shakes his head and tries to pass, but the white man steps in his way and repeats what is now a challenge to the man's very presence in the building: "Can I *help* you?" Only then does the partner reveal his identity to the young man, who then steps aside to let him pass. The young white man had no reason to assume the right to control the older man standing before him, except the reason provided by the cultural assumption of white racial dominance that can override any class advantage a person of color might have.[14]

The milder forms of unearned advantage usually change first because they are the easiest for privileged groups to give up. Over the last several decades, for example, national surveys show a steady decline in the percentage of whites in the United States who express overtly racist attitudes toward people of color. This trend is reflected in diversity training programs that usually focus on appreciating or at least tolerating differences—in other words, extending unearned entitlements to everyone instead of the dominant group alone.

It's much harder, however, to do something about power and the unequal distribution of resources and rewards. This is why issues of conferred dominance and the stronger forms of unearned advantage get much less attention, and why, when they are raised, they often provoke hostile defensiveness, especially from those who struggle with a lack of class privilege. Perhaps more than any other factor, this reluctance to come to terms with more serious and entrenched forms of privilege is why most diversity programs produce limited and short-lived results.

What Privilege Looks Like in Everyday Life

As Peggy McIntosh showed in her groundbreaking work,[15] privilege shows up in the daily details of people's lives in almost every social setting. Consider the following examples of race privilege.[16] This is a long list because the details of people's lives are many and varied. Resist the temptation to go through it quickly. Take your time and try to identify situations in which each might occur. As you read these lists, you may find yourself wondering why you should believe that any of this material is true, especially if you're white or male or heterosexual or nondisabled. Since I'm all those things, let me tell you why I believe it.

Some of the items are based on scientifically gathered data, such as income statistics or studies of everything from access to health care to bias in the criminal justice system to how much people pay for cars. Other items are based on the enormous weight of evidence compiled over many years in the stories that people tell about their experience living in this society. Added to this is the logic of understanding what is most likely to happen in a world organized as this one is. This doesn't qualify as scientific proof, but many things we know to be true are not scientifically provable in the strictest sense. For example, I cannot prove scientifically that being a slave on a plantation was a terrible experience. But I can show lots of evidence that supports this claim—stories of slaves and former slaves, diaries of slave holders, photographs of slaves who were horribly scarred from being whipped, newspaper stories from slavery times, and so on. I can also imagine what it would be like to live under such conditions. Putting all this evidence together, it's safe to conclude that it must have been terrible, even though, strictly speaking, I can't prove it.

What follows, then, is not simply a matter of personal opinion. It is supported by a great deal of evidence of various kinds gathered over many years. If you want to see for yourself, go to the "Resources" section at the end of the book.

- Whites are less likely than blacks to be arrested; once arrested, they are less likely to be convicted and, once convicted, less likely to go to prison, regardless of the crime or circumstances. Whites, for example, constitute 85 percent of those who use illegal drugs, but less than half of those in prison on drug-use charges are white.

■ Although many superstar professional athletes are black, in general black players are held to higher standards than whites. It is easier for a "good but not great" white player to make a professional team than it is for a similar black.

■ Whites are more likely than comparable blacks to have loan applications approved and less likely to be given poor information or the runaround during the application process.

■ Whites are charged lower prices for new and used cars than are people of color, and residential segregation gives whites access to higher-quality goods of all kinds at cheaper prices.

■ Whites can choose whether to be conscious of their racial identity or to ignore it and regard themselves as simply human beings without a race.

■ Whites are more likely to control conversations and be allowed to get away with it and to have their ideas and contributions taken seriously, including those that were suggested previously by a person of color and ignored or dismissed.

■ Whites can usually assume that national heroes, success models, and other figures held up for general admiration will be of their race.

■ Whites can generally assume that when they go out in public, they won't be challenged and asked to explain what they're doing, nor will they be attacked by hate groups simply because of their race.

■ Whites can assume that when they go shopping, they'll be treated as serious customers not as potential shoplifters or people without the money to make a purchase. When they try to cash a check or use a credit card, they can assume they won't be hassled for additional identification and will be given the benefit of the doubt.

■ White representation in government and the ruling circles of corporations, universities, and other organizations is disproportionately high.

■ Most whites are not segregated into communities that isolate them from the best job opportunities, schools, and community services.

- Whites have greater access to quality education and health care.

- Whites are more likely to be given early opportunities to show what they can do at work, to be identified as potential candidates for promotion, to be mentored, to be given a second chance when they fail, and to be allowed to treat failure as a learning experience rather than as an indication of who they are and the shortcomings of their race.

- Whites can assume that race won't be used to predict whether they'll fit in at work or whether teammates will feel comfortable working with them.

- Whites can succeed without other people being surprised.

- Whites don't have to deal with an endless and exhausting stream of attention to their race. They can simply take their race for granted as unremarkable to the extent of experiencing themselves as not even having a race. Unlike some of my African American students, for example, I don't have people coming up to me and treating me as if I were some exotic "other," gushing about how "cool" or different I am, wanting to know where I'm "from," and reaching out to touch my hair.

- Whites don't find themselves slotted into occupations identified with their race, as blacks are often slotted into support positions or Asians into technical jobs.

- Whites aren't confused with other whites, as if all whites look alike. They're noticed for their individuality, and they take offense whenever they're put in a category (such as "white") rather than perceived and treated as individuals.

- Whites can reasonably expect that if they work hard and "play by the rules," they'll get what they deserve, and they feel justified in complaining if they don't. It is something other racial groups cannot realistically expect.

In the following list for male privilege, note how some items repeat from the list on race but other items do not.

- In most professions and upper-level occupations, men are held to a lower standard than women. It is easier for a "good but not great" male lawyer to make partner than it is for a comparable woman.

- Men are charged lower prices for new and used cars.

- If men do poorly at something or make a mistake or commit a crime, they can generally assume that people won't attribute the failure to their gender. The kids who shoot teachers and schoolmates are almost always boys, but rarely is the fact that all this violence is being done by males raised as an important issue.

- Men can usually assume that national heroes, success models, and other figures held up for general admiration will be men.

- Men can generally assume that when they go out in public, they won't be sexually harassed or assaulted just because they're male, and if they are victimized, they won't be asked to explain what they were doing there.

- Male representation in government and the ruling circles of corporations and other organizations is disproportionately high.

- Men are more likely to be given early opportunities to show what they can do at work, to be identified as potential candidates for promotion, to be mentored, to be given a second chance when they fail, and to be allowed to treat failure as a learning experience rather than as an indication of who they are and the shortcomings of their gender.

- Men are more likely than women are to control conversations and be allowed to get away with it and to have their ideas and contributions taken seriously, even those that were suggested previously by a woman and dismissed or ignored.

- Most men can assume that their gender won't be used to determine whether they'll fit in at work or whether teammates will feel comfortable working with them.

- Men can succeed without other people being surprised.

- Men don't have to deal with an endless and exhausting stream of attention drawn to their gender (for example, to how sexually attractive they are).

- Men don't find themselves slotted into a narrow range of occupations identified with their gender as women are slotted into community relations, human resources, social work, elementary school teaching, librarianship, nursing, and clerical, and secretarial positions.

▪ Men can reasonably expect that if they work hard and "play by the rules," they'll get what they deserve and feel justified in complaining if they don't.

▪ The standards used to evaluate men as *men* are consistent with the standards used to evaluate them in other roles such as occupations. Standards used to evaluate women as women are often different from those used to evaluate them in other roles. For example, a man can be both a "real man" and a successful and aggressive lawyer, while an aggressive woman lawyer may succeed as a lawyer but be judged as not measuring up as a woman.

In the following list regarding sexual orientation, note again items in common with the other two lists and items peculiar to this form of privilege.

▪ Heterosexuals are free to reveal and live their intimate relationships openly—by referring to their partners by name, recounting experiences, going out in public together, displaying pictures on their desks at work—without being accused of "flaunting" their sexuality or risking discrimination.

▪ Heterosexuals can marry as a way to commit to long-term relationships that are socially recognized, supported, and legitimated. This fact confers basic rights such as spousal health benefits, the ability to adopt children, inheritance, joint filing of income tax returns, and the power to make decisions for a spouse who is incapacitated in a medical emergency.

▪ Heterosexuals can rest assured that whether they're hired, promoted, or fired from a job will have nothing to do with their sexual orientation, an aspect of themselves they cannot change.

▪ Heterosexuals can move about in public without fear of being harassed or physically attacked because of their sexual orientation.

▪ Heterosexuals don't run the risk of being reduced to a single aspect of their lives, as if being heterosexual summed up the kind of person they are. Instead, they can be viewed and treated as complex human beings who happen to be heterosexual.

- Heterosexuals can usually assume that national heroes, success models, and other figures held up for general admiration will be assumed to be heterosexual.

- Most heterosexuals can assume that their sexual orientation won't be used to determine whether they'll fit in at work or whether teammates will feel comfortable working with them.

- Heterosexuals don't have to worry that their sexual orientation will be used as a weapon against them, to undermine their achievements or power.

- Heterosexuals can turn on the television or go to the movies and be assured of seeing characters, news reports, and stories that reflect the reality of their lives.

- Heterosexuals can live where they want without having to worry about neighbors who disapprove of their sexual orientation.

- Heterosexuals can live in the comfort of knowing that other people's assumptions about their sexual orientation are correct.

In the following list regarding disability status, note again items in common with the other lists and items peculiar to this form of privilege.

- Nondisabled people can choose whether to be conscious of their disability status or to ignore it and regard themselves simply as human beings.

- Nondisabled people can live secure in other people's assumption that they are sexual beings capable of an active sex life, including the potential to have children and be parents.

- Nondisabled people have greater access to education and health care. They are less likely to be singled out based on stereotypes that underestimate their abilities and be put in "special education" classes that don't allow them to develop their full potential.

- Nondisabled people can assume that they will fit in at work and in other settings without having to worry about being evaluated and judged according to preconceived notions and stereotypes about people with disabilities.

- Nondisabled people are more likely to be given early opportunities to show what they can do at work, to be identified as potential candidates for promotion, to be mentored, to be given a second chance when they fail, and to be allowed to treat failure as a learning experience rather than as an indication of who they are.

- Nondisabled people don't have to deal with an endless and exhausting stream of attention to their disability status. They can simply take their disability status for granted as unremarkable to the extent of experiencing themselves as not even having one.

- Nondisabled people can ask for help without having to worry that people will assume they need help with everything.

- Nondisabled people can succeed without people being surprised because of low expectations of their ability to contribute to society.

- Nondisabled people can expect to pay lower prices for cars because they are assumed to be mentally unimpaired and less likely to allow themselves to be misled and exploited.

- Nondisabled people can assume that if they work hard and play by the rules, they'll get what they deserve without having to overcome stereotypes about their ability status. They are less likely to be shuttled into dead-end, menial jobs, given inadequate job training, paid less than they are worth regardless of their ability, and separated from workers unlike themselves.

- Nondisabled people are more likely to control conversations and be allowed to get away with it and have their ideas and contributions taken seriously, including those that were suggested before by a person with disabilities and then dismissed or ignored.

- Nondisabled people can assume that national heroes, success models, and other figures held up for general admiration will share their disability status.

- Nondisabled people can go to polling places on election day knowing they will have access to voting machines that allow them to exercise their rights as citizens in privacy without the assistance of others.

- Nondisabled people can generally assume that when they go out in public, they won't be looked at as odd or out of place or not belonging. They can also assume that most buildings and other structures will not be designed in ways that limit their access.

- Nondisabled people can assume that when they need to travel from one place to another, they will have access to buses, trains, airplanes, and other means of transportation.

- Nondisabled people can count on being taken seriously and not treated as children.

- Nondisabled people are less likely to be segregated into living situations—such as nursing homes and special schools and sports programs—that isolate them from job opportunities, schools, community services, and the everyday workings of life in a society.

- Nondisabled people don't have to worry about their disability status being used against them when trying to fit in at work or whether teammates will feel comfortable working with them.

As data from the U.S. Census and other sources show, one of the most visible consequences of privilege is the uneven distribution of jobs, wealth, and income and all that goes with it, from decent housing and good schools to adequate health care. At every level of education, for example, whites are half as likely as are people of color to be unemployed or have incomes below the poverty line. The average white household has more than 14 times the net wealth of the average African American household, and the average annual income for whites who work year-round and full-time is 44 percent greater than it is for comparable African Americans. It is 60 percent greater than for Latinas and Latinos. The white income advantage exists at all levels of educational attainment.[17]

As to gender inequality, men who work year-round and full-time earn on average 50 percent more than do comparable women.[18]

Compared with people who have disabilities, nondisabled people are twice as likely to complete high school and college, more than twice as likely to be employed, and half as likely to live in poverty.[19]

Regardless of which group we're talking about, privilege generally allows people to assume a certain level of acceptance, inclusion, and respect in the world, to operate within a relatively wide comfort zone. Privilege increases the odds of having things your own way, of being able to set the agenda in a social situation and determine the rules and standards and how they're applied. Privilege grants the cultural authority to make judgments about others and to have those judgments stick. It allows people to define reality and to have prevailing definitions of reality fit their experience. Privilege means being able to decide who gets taken seriously, who receives attention, who is accountable to whom and for what. And it grants a presumption of superiority and social permission to act on that presumption without having to worry about being challenged.

To have privilege is to be allowed to move through your life without being marked in ways that identify you as an outsider, as exceptional or "other" to be excluded, or to be included but always with conditions. As Paul Kivel points out, "In the United States, a person is considered a member of the lowest status group from which they have any heritage."[20] This means that if you come from several ethnic groups, the one that lowers your status is the one you're most likely to be tagged with, as in "She's part Jewish" or "He's part Vietnamese" but rarely "She's part white." In fact, as we saw earlier, having any black ancestry is still enough to be classified as *entirely* black in many people's eyes. People are tagged with other labels that point to the lowest-status group they belong to, as in "woman doctor" or "black writer" but never "white lawyer" or "male senator." Any category that lowers our status relative to others' can be used to mark us; to be privileged is to go through life with the relative ease of being unmarked.[21]

As I'm using the term *privilege* here, I distinguish it from good luck or being able to do things that one personally values but that aren't valued in the culture. Having good friends, for example, is both lucky and good, but it's not a form of privilege unless it is systematically allowed for some and denied to others based on membership in social categories. Nor is something such as feeling free to express emotion a form of privilege, even though many people consider it a good thing and something that's allowed for women and discouraged in men. The reason emotional expressiveness isn't a privilege is that although it may be good for health and well-being, patriarchal culture puts a low value on it compared with appearing to be tough and always being in control as

core aspects of patriarchal masculinity. Privilege is a feature of social systems, and something that isn't highly valued in the culture of a system
can never qualify as a form of privilege. I may personally be glad that I
feel free to have a good cry when I need to, but it's hard to think of a
situation in which doing so would elevate my status. It's easy, however,
to think of situations in which it would have just the opposite effect.

If you're male or heterosexual or white or nondisabled and you
find yourself shaking your head at the foregoing descriptions of privilege—"This isn't true for *me*"—it might be due to the complex and
sometimes paradoxical way that privilege works in social life.

PRIVILEGE AS PARADOX

One of the paradoxes of privilege is that although it is received *by*
individuals, the granting of privilege has nothing to do with who
those individuals are as people. Instead, individuals receive privilege
only because they are perceived by others as belonging to privileged
groups and social categories. In other words, male privilege is more
about *male* people than it is about male *people*. I don't have privilege
because of who I am as a person. Maleness is privileged in this
society, and I have male privilege only when people identify me as
belonging to the category "male." I do or don't receive privilege based
on which category people put me in without their knowing a single
other thing about me.

This means that you don't actually have to be male, for example,
to receive the privilege attached to that category. All you have to do
is convince people you belong to the appropriate category. The film
Shakespeare in Love, for example, is set in Elizabethan England, where
acting on the stage was a privilege reserved for men. The character
Viola (the woman Shakespeare falls in love with) wants more than anything to act on the stage and finally realizes her dream, not by changing her sex and becoming a man but by successfully presenting herself as one. That's all it takes. In similar ways, gays and lesbians can
have access to heterosexual privilege so long as they don't reveal their
sexual orientation. And people with hidden disabilities such as
epilepsy, many diseases, and learning disabilities can receive nondisabled privilege so long as they do not disclose their disability status.

You can also lose privilege if people think you *don't* belong to a particular category. My sexual orientation is heterosexual, which entitles me to heterosexual privilege, but only if people identify me as such. If I were to announce to everyone that I'm gay, I would immediately lose my access to heterosexual privilege (unless people refused to believe me), even though I would still be, in fact, heterosexual. As Charlotte Bunch put it, "If you don't have a sense of what privilege is, I suggest that you go home and announce to everybody that you know—a roommate, your family, the people you work with—that you're a queer. Try being queer for a week."[22] When it comes to privilege, then, it doesn't really matter who we really are. What matters is who other people *think* we are, which is to say, the social categories they put us in.

Several important consequences follow from this paradox of privilege. First, privilege is rooted in societies and groups as much as it's rooted in people's personalities and how they perceive and react to one another. This means that doing something about the problem of privilege takes more than changing individuals. As Harry Brod wrote about male privilege:

> We need to be clear that there is no such thing as giving up one's privilege to be "outside" the system. One is always *in* the system. The only question is whether one is part of the system in a way which challenges or strengthens the status quo. Privilege is not something I *take* and which I therefore have the option of *not* taking. It is something that society *gives* me, and unless I change the institutions which give it to me, they will continue to give it, and I will continue to *have* it, however noble and egalitarian my intentions.[23]

Social systems and the people who make them happen promote privilege in complicated ways, which we'll look at in later chapters. For now, be aware that we don't have to be special or even feel special in order to have access to privilege, because privilege doesn't derive from who we are or what we've done. It is, as we've seen, a social arrangement that depends on which category we happen to be sorted into by other people and how they treat us as a result.

The paradoxical experience of *being* privileged without *feeling* privileged is a second consequence of the fact that privilege is more about social categories than who people are. It has to do primarily with the people we use as standards of comparison—what sociologists call "reference groups." We use reference groups to construct a sense of how good or bad, high or low we are in the scheme of things. To do this, we usually don't look downward in the social hierarchy but to people we identify as being on the same level as or higher level than our own. So pointing out to someone who lives in poverty in the United States that they're better off than are many people in India doesn't make them feel better, because people in the United States don't use Indians as a reference group. Instead, they will compare themselves with those who seem like them in key respects and see if they're doing better or worse than *those people* are.

Since being white is valued in this society, whites tend to compare themselves with other whites, not with people of color. In the same way, men tend to compare themselves with other men and not with women. What this means, however, is that whites tend not to feel privileged *by their race* when they compare themselves with their reference group, because their reference group is also white. In the same way, men don't feel privileged *by their gender* in comparison with other men, because gender doesn't elevate them above other *men*. A partial exception to this is the hierarchy that exists among men between heterosexuals and gays, by which heterosexual men are more likely to consider themselves "real men" and therefore socially valued above gay men. But even here, the mere fact of being male isn't experienced as a form of privilege, because gay men are also male.

An exception to these patterns can occur for those who are privileged by gender or race but find themselves ranked low in terms of social class. To protect themselves from feeling and being seen as on the bottom of the ladder, they may go out of their way to compare themselves to women or people of color by emphasizing their supposed gender or racial superiority. This can appear as an exaggerated sense of masculinity, for example, or as overt attempts to put women or people of color "in their place" by harassment, violence, or behavior that is openly contemptuous or demeaning.

A corollary to being privileged without knowing it is to be on the *other* side of privilege without necessarily feeling *that*. For example, I sometimes hear a woman say something like, "I've never been oppressed as a woman." Often this is said to challenge the idea that male privilege exists at all. But this confuses the social position of females and males as social categories with one woman's subjective experience of belonging to one of those categories. They are not the same. For various reasons—including class privilege or an unusual family experience or simply being young—she may have avoided exposure to many of the consequences of being female in a society that privileges maleness. Or she may have managed to overcome them to a degree that she doesn't feel hampered by them. Or she may be engaging in denial. Or she may be unaware of how she is discriminated against (unaware, perhaps, that being a woman is the reason her professors ignore her in class) or may have so internalized her subordinate status that she doesn't see it as a problem (thinking, perhaps, that women are ignored because they aren't intelligent enough to say anything worth listening to). Regardless of what her experience is based on, it is just that—her experience—and it doesn't have to square with the larger social reality that everyone (including her) must deal with one way or another. It's like living in a rainy climate and somehow avoiding being rained on yourself. It's still a rainy place to be, and getting wet is something most people have to deal with.

The Paradox That Privilege Doesn't Necessarily Make You Happy

I often hear men deny the existence of male privilege by saying they don't feel happy or fulfilled in their own lives. They reason that you can't be both privileged and miserable, or, as one man put it, "Privilege means 'having all the goodies,'" so if you don't feel good, then you must not be privileged.

This is a common reaction that is related to the difference between individuals and social categories. Knowing that someone belongs to one or more of the privileged categories, "white," or "heterosexual," or "male," or "nondisabled" doesn't tell us what life is actually like for them. Belonging to a privileged category improves the odds in favor of certain kinds of advantages and preferential treatment, but it doesn't guarantee anything for any given individual. Being born white, male, and upper-class, for example, is a powerful combination of privileged categories that would certainly put a person in line for all kinds of valued things. But this person could still wind up losing it all in the stock market and living under a bridge in a cardboard box. Nonetheless, even though the privilege attached to race, gender, and social class didn't work out for this particular person, the privilege itself still exists as a fact of social life.

Another reason privilege and happiness often don't go together is that privilege can exact a cost from those who have it. To have privilege is to participate in a system that confers advantage and dominance at the expense of other people, and this situation can cause distress to those who benefit from it. White privilege, for example, comes at a huge cost to people of color, and on some level white people must struggle with this knowledge. That's where all the guilt comes from and the lengths to which white people will often go to avoid feeling and looking at it. In similar ways, male privilege exacts a cost as men compete with other men and strive to prove their manhood so they can be counted among "real men" who are worthy of being set apart from—and above—women. It should therefore come as no surprise that men often feel unhappy and that they associate their unhappiness with the fact of being men.

OPPRESSION: THE FLIP SIDE OF PRIVILEGE

For every social category that is privileged, one or more other categories are oppressed in relation to it. As Marilyn Frye described it, the concept of oppression points to social forces that tend to "press" on people and hold them down, to hem them in and block their pursuit of a good life. Just as privilege tends to open doors of opportunity, oppression tends to slam them shut.[24]

Like privilege, oppression results from the social relationship between privileged and oppressed categories, which makes it possible for individuals to vary in their personal experience of being oppressed ("I've never been oppressed as a woman"). This also means, however, that in order to have the experience of being oppressed, it is necessary to belong to an oppressed category. In other words, men cannot be oppressed *as men*, just as whites cannot be oppressed as whites or heterosexuals as heterosexuals, because a group can be oppressed only if there exists another group with the power to oppress them.

As we saw earlier, people in privileged categories can certainly feel bad in ways that can feel oppressive. Men, for example, can feel burdened by what they take to be their responsibility to provide for their families. Or they can feel limited and even damaged by the requirement that "real men" must avoid expressing feelings other than anger. But although access to privilege costs them something that may *feel* oppressive, to call it oppression distorts the nature of what is happening to them and why.

It ignores, for example, the fact that the cost of male privilege is far outweighed by the benefits, while the oppressive cost of being female is not outweighed by corresponding benefits. Misapplying the label of "oppression" also tempts us into the false argument that if men and women are *both* oppressed because of gender, then one oppression balances out the other and no privilege can be said to exist. So, when we try to label the pain that men feel because of gender (or that whites feel because of racism, and so on), whether we call it "oppression" or simply "pain" makes a huge difference in how we perceive the world and how it works.

The complexity of systems of privilege makes it possible, of course, for men to experience oppression if they also happen to be of color or gay or disabled or in a lower social class, but not simply because they are male. In the same way, whites can experience oppression for many reasons, but not because they're white.

Note also that because oppression results from relations between social categories, it is not possible to be oppressed by society itself. Living in a particular society can make people feel miserable, but we can't call that misery "oppression" unless it arises from being on the losing end in a system of privilege. That can't happen in relation to society as a whole, because a society isn't something that can have privilege. Only people can do this by belonging to privileged categories in relation to other categories that aren't.

Finally, being in a privileged category that has an oppressive relationship with another isn't the same as being an oppressive *person* who behaves in oppressive ways. That males as a social category oppress females as a social category, for example, is a social fact. That doesn't, however, tell us how a particular man thinks or feels about particular women or behaves toward them. This can be a subtle distinction to hang on to, but hang on to it we must if we're going to maintain a clear idea of what oppression is and how it works in defense of privilege.

Now that we're getting into the pervasiveness of the damage of privilege and oppression in people's lives, we may feel helpless and wonder, "What can anyone do about it?" If you find yourself feeling that way now or later on, turn to Chapter 9, which is devoted to that question.

CHAPTER 3

Capitalism, Class,
and the Matrix of Domination

Whenever I teach about race, there always comes a point when students start saying things such as "We don't get it. If race is socially constructed and doesn't exist otherwise, and if human beings don't have to be afraid of one another, then where does racism come from? Why all the oppression and hostility and violence over something that's made up? And why would people make it up this way in the first place? It's stupid."

The answer takes us into the history of race, where we find two things that usually startle students as much as they did me when I first became aware of them. First, white racism hasn't been around very long—hardly more than several centuries and certainly not as long as peoples now considered "white" have been aware of other "races." Second, its appearance in Europe and the Americas occurred right along with the expansion of capitalism as an economic system. This is no coincidence, because capitalism played a major role in the development of white privilege and still plays a major role in its perpetuation.

This isn't surprising given the importance of economics in social life, which is, after all, how people organize themselves to provide what they need for their material existence—food, shelter, clothing, and the like—and to live what their culture defines as a "good life." Because economic systems are the source of wealth, they are also the basis for every social institution, since the state and church and universities and the like cannot survive without an economic base. It takes a great deal of material and labor to build a cathedral or a university, for example, or to pay for political campaigns or equip and feed a police force or an army. This means that the central place of economics in social life gives individuals and systems powerful reasons to go along with the dominant economic system. Capitalism has been that system for the last several hundred years, and since the demise of the Soviet Union, it's virtually the only game in town.

What, then, did capitalism have to do with the origins of white racism? In the simplest sense, it was a matter of economics. Understanding why begins with understanding capitalism itself.[1]

HOW CAPITALISM WORKS

The basic goal of modern capitalism is to turn money into more money. Capitalists invest money to buy what it takes to produce goods and services—raw materials, machinery, electricity, buildings, and, of course, human labor. It doesn't matter what they produce so long as they can find a market in which to sell it at a profit—for more than it cost to have it produced—and end up with more money than they started with. Whether the result enhances human life (providing food, affordable housing, health care, and the like) or causes harm (tobacco, alcohol, drugs, weapons, slavery, pollution) may be an issue for individual capitalists who value a clear conscience. But the system itself doesn't depend on such moral or ethical considerations, because profit is profit and there's no way to tell "good" money from "bad." Even the damage done by one enterprise can serve as a source of profit for another, as when industrial pollution creates opportunities for companies that specialize in cleaning it up.

Capitalists employ workers to produce goods and services, paying them wages in exchange for their time. Capitalists then sell the goods and services that workers produce. For capitalists to make a living (since they don't produce anything themselves), they have to get workers to produce goods and services that are worth more than the wages capitalists pay them. The difference is what capitalists live on.

Why, however, would workers accept wages worth less than the value of what they produce? The general answer is that they don't have much choice, because under capitalism the tools and factories used to produce goods aren't owned by the people who actually do the work. Instead, they're owned by capitalists, especially stockholders who invest in companies. So, for most people who want to earn a living, chances are they'll have to work for one capitalist employer or another, which means choosing between working on the capitalist's terms or not working at all. As corporate capitalism has extended its reach into every area of social life, even professionals now have to confront this choice. Physicians, for example, who were once regarded as the model of an independent profession, are increasingly compelled to become what are essentially highly paid employees of health maintenance organizations. As a result, some have lobbied Congress for the right to engage in collective bargaining with HMOs—in other words, to form a labor union for physicians.[2]

Since capitalists profit from the difference between the cost of producing goods (most of which is people's labor) and what they can sell goods for in markets, the cheaper the labor, the more money left over for them. This is why capitalists are so concerned about increasing "worker productivity"—finding ways for workers to produce more goods for the same or less pay. One way to accomplish this is through the use of technology, especially machines that replace people altogether. Another is to threaten to close down or relocate businesses if workers won't make concessions on wages, health and retirement benefits, job security, and working conditions. A third and increasingly popular strategy in the "new global economy" is to move production to countries where people are willing to work for less than they are in Europe or North America and where authoritarian governments control workers and discourage the formation of unions and other sources of organized resistance, often with the direct support of the U.S. government.[3]

CAPITALISM AND CLASS

The dynamics of capitalism produce not only enormous amounts of wealth but high—and increasing—levels of inequality, both within societies and globally. The richest 10 percent of the U.S. population holds more than two-thirds of all the wealth, including almost 90 percent of cash, almost half the land, more than 90 percent of business assets, and almost all stocks and bonds.[4] The richest top 20 percent of all households receives 56 percent of all income, and the richest 40 percent receives 78 percent, leaving less than a quarter of all income to be divided among the remaining 60 percent of all households.[5]

Such patterns of inequality result from and perpetuate a class system based on widening gaps in income, wealth, and power between those on top and everyone below them.[6] It is a system that produces oppressive consequences. For those at the bottom, the costs are enormous, with living conditions among the rural poor, for example, at or below the level found in many of the world's most impoverished nonindustrial societies.[7] Even among employed members of the working class, as well as many of those in the middle class, the class system offers little security and takes an emotional toll. A great many jobs are boring, mind-numbing, and make use of much less than what most people have to offer. And the vast majority of working people have little if any control over the work they do or whether they keep their jobs.

It also doesn't take much to see that with the bottom 60 percent of the U.S. population having to divide less than a quarter of all income among themselves, there isn't going to be enough to go around. While capitalism produces an overall abundance of goods and services, it distributes that wealth so unequally that it also produces conditions of scarcity for most of the population. This makes life for those 175 million or so people an ongoing competition that is full of anxiety and struggle. For a majority of people, it wouldn't take very much—a divorce, perhaps, or a serious illness or being laid off—to substantially lower their standard of living, even to the extent of putting them out of their homes and onto welfare.[8]

The "American Dream" aside, most people also have relatively little power to improve their class position.[9] Much of the increase in household wealth, for example, has been based on a growing mountain of credit card debt, people working two or more jobs, and families relying on two wage earners to support the same standard of living their parents managed with one. Although unemployment is low, most of the new jobs that have been created over the last several decades have been low-paying and with little chance of advancement. In addition, studies of occupational mobility show most people are as likely to move downward as they are upward in the class system. Because of this and the widening gulf separating the upper class from everyone else, the middle class has shrunk.[10] Since 1964, the percentage of people who see themselves as middle class has fallen from 61 to 46, while the percentage seeing themselves as working class has risen from 35 to 45.[11]

In short, in an era of continuing corporate downsizing, the flight of well-paying industrial jobs overseas, and the rapid growth of low-level service occupations, for most people the struggle to move upward rarely gets much beyond hanging on to what they have.[12] There is, of course, upward movement by some, but excluding high-technology fields that are currently in demand, this almost always comes at the expense of others who must move down to make room for them. This situation creates what economist Lester Thurow calls a "zero-sum" society, adapting a term used to describe games that are designed so that one person's gain is always someone else's loss.[13] Thus it is inevitable that at any given moment a substantial proportion of the population will have to live in poverty or close to it and that different groups within the "bottom" 60 percent will see one another as competitors and threats to their livelihood.

As we'll see below, such dynamics of capitalism have played a key role in the trouble surrounding privilege, especially in relation to race and gender.

CAPITALISM, DIFFERENCE, AND PRIVILEGE: RACE AND GENDER

Given how capitalism works, it connects to white racism in ways that are both direct and indirect. In the history of the United States, the direct connection is most apparent in the enslavement of millions of Africans as a source of cheap labor on cotton and tobacco plantations in the South. This was done for purely economic reasons, as became dramatically apparent after Eli Whitney's invention of the cotton gin in 1792 made it possible to process far more cotton than before. Tempted by the potential to multiply cotton production—and profits— many times over, planters chose to minimize labor costs by exploiting slave labor rather than pay free workers a living wage. As a result, the number of enslaved blacks in the United States jumped from 1 million in 1800 to almost 4 million in 1860, just before the start of the Civil War.[14] The primacy of profit in white thinking was also apparent in the reactions of businesses that relied on paid white workers. They didn't object to slavery on moral grounds. Instead, they complained that slave owners were engaging in unfair competition because their labor costs were so low it was impossible to compete against them. It was common, for example, for construction firms that depended on slave labor to win contracts away from their competition by underbidding them.[15]

Following the Civil War, the capitalist appetite for cheap agricultural labor was no less than before, and freed blacks were held in a new form of bondage by an oppressive system of tenant farming that kept them perpetually in debt.[16] Beyond the South, the profitability of racism showed itself in the widespread use of Chinese immigrant labor to build the Western railways under harsh and demeaning conditions. Even farther west, Japanese immigrants had similar experiences on the sugar and pineapple plantations of Hawaii.[17]

Capitalism's direct connection to white racism has also operated in the acquisition of land and raw materials, which, like cheap labor, play a key role in the rapid growth of industry and wealth. In the heyday of capitalist expansion during the eighteenth and nineteenth centuries, Europe and then the United States found an abundance of what they needed in Africa, Asia, and the Americas. To acquire it, they relied on varying combinations of military conquest, political domination, and economic exploitation.[18] They were spectacularly successful at it, especially Great Britain, a small island nation with few natural resources of its own that nonetheless managed to become the world's first true industrial power. Unlike Britain, the United States was already rich in natural resources, but whites could get at them only by taking them away from the Native American tribes who inhabited most of the land, as well as from Mexico, which encompassed most of what is now the far western and southwestern United States. Whites managed to take what they wanted through a combination of conquest, genocide, and a complex array of treaties that were routinely ignored.[19]

To justify such direct forms of imperialism and oppression, whites developed the *idea* of whiteness to define a privileged social category elevated above everyone who wasn't included in it.[20] This made it possible to reconcile conquest, treachery, slavery, and genocide with the nation's newly professed ideals of democracy, freedom, and human dignity. If whiteness defined what it meant to be human, then it was seen as less of an offense against the Constitution (not to mention God) to dominate and oppress those who happened to fall outside that definition as the United States marched onward toward what was popularly perceived as its Manifest Destiny.[21]

Other capitalist connections to racism have been less direct. Capitalists, for example, have often used racism as a strategy to control white workers and thereby keep wages low and productivity high. This has been done in two ways. First, beginning early in the nineteenth century, there was a systematic campaign to encourage white workers to adopt whiteness as a key part of their social identity—something they hadn't done before—and to accept the supposed superiority of whiteness as compensation for their low class position. No matter how badly treated they were by their employers, they could always look in the mirror and comfort themselves with the fact of being white and therefore elevated above people of color, even those who might have a class position higher than their own.[22] With the emancipation of the slaves following the Civil War, however, lower-class whites could no longer point to their freedom as a mark of superiority. The response to this loss was a period of enormous violence and intimidation directed at blacks, much of which was perpetrated by the newly formed Ku Klux Klan, with no serious opposition from government or the larger white population.

Another way for capitalists to control workers is to keep them worried over the possibility of losing their jobs if they demand higher wages or better working conditions. Racism has a long history of being used in this way. The oppressed condition of blacks and other racial minorities encourages them to work for wages that are lower than what most whites will accept. Employers have used this to pose an ongoing threat to white workers who have known employers could readily use racial minorities as an inexpensive replacement for them. This has worked most effectively as a way to break strikes and the labor unions that promote them. As unions became more powerful at the turn of the twentieth century, for example, employers often brought in black workers as strikebreakers. The strategy worked to draw the attention of white workers away from issues of capitalism and class to issues of race. It focused their fear and anger on the supposed threat from black workers, which made them less likely to see their common condition as workers and join together against the capitalists. In this way, racial division and conflict became an effective strategy for dividing different segments of the working class against one another.[23]

Similar dynamics operate today, although perhaps with greater subtlety. The controversy over affirmative action programs, for example, as well as the influx of immigrant workers from Mexico and Asia and the "outsourcing" of jobs to other countries, all reflect an underlying belief that the greatest challenge facing white workers is unfair competition from people of color both here and abroad. This belief ignores the capitalist system itself, which by its nature increases the wealth of capitalists by controlling workers and keeping wages as low as possible, and it allows a small elite to control the vast majority of wealth and income, leaving a relatively small share to be divided among everyone else. Such dynamics of capitalism make for conditions of scarcity that encourage fierce competition, especially in the working and lower classes but also in many segments of the middle class.

Given the historical legacy that encourages whites to feel a sense of superiority and entitlement in relation to people of color, such competition is bound to provoke anger and resentment among whites, which is then directed at people of color rather than at those whose wealth and power lie at the heart of what is essentially an economic problem centering on the distribution of wealth. In this way, dynamics of class privilege fuel continued racism, which, in turn, draws attention away from capitalism and the class oppression it produces. The result, as Michael Reich shows, is that white racism actually hurts white workers by strengthening the position of capitalists at white workers' expense.[24]

Capitalism exploits people with disabilities through "sheltered workshops" in nonprofit organizations such as Goodwill Industries and Lighthouse for the Blind that secured for themselves an exception to the 1938 minimum wage law to enable them to hire people with disabilities at less than minimum wages. Working conditions separate workers with disabilities from nondisabled workers, place them under the supervision of nondisabled people, and provide little opportunity for challenge or advancement.[25]

Capitalism also shapes and makes use of gender inequality.[26] The cultural devaluing of women, for example, has long been used as an excuse to pay them less and exploit them as a source of cheap labor, whether in the corporate secretarial pool in New York or garment sweatshops in Los Angeles or electronics industry assembly plants in Asia.[27] Women's supposed inferiority has also been used as a basis for the belief that much of the work that women do isn't work at all and therefore isn't worthy of anything more than emotional compensation.[28] Capitalism couldn't function without the army of women who do the shopping for households (which is how most goods are purchased) and do the labor through which those goods are consumed—cooking the meals, making the bed with the new set of sheets, and so on. On a deeper level, women are, with few exceptions, the ones who nurture and raise each new generation of workers on which capitalism depends, and this vital service is provided without anyone's having to pay wages or provide health and retirement benefits. Women do it for free—even when they also work outside the home—to the benefit of the capitalist system and those who are most privileged by it.

Capitalism, then, provides an important social context for the trouble that surrounds privilege. And the class dynamics that arise from capitalism interact with that trouble in powerful ways that both protect capitalism and class privilege and perpetuate privilege and oppression based on difference.

THE MATRIX OF DOMINATION AND THE PARADOX OF BEING PRIVILEGED AND UNPRIVILEGED AT THE SAME TIME

As the dynamics of capitalism and class suggest, systems of privilege are complicated. This is one reason why people can belong to a privileged category and not feel privileged. There is more than one set of categories, which means a person can belong to the privileged category in one set and an unprivileged category in another. So, for example, a middle-class white lesbian's class and race privilege may blind her to issues of race and class, or her experience of gender inequality and heterosexism may foster the illusion that this automatically prepares her to know everything she needs to know about other forms of privilege and oppression. Or a working-class white man may be annoyed by the idea that his whiteness and maleness somehow give him access to privilege. As a member of the working class, he may feel so pushed around and looked down on that the last thing that he feels is privileged.

Part of such feelings comes from the misconception that privilege is something that is just about individuals. From that perspective, either he's privileged or he's not, just like either he has two ears or he doesn't. If he can show that he's not privileged in some way (being working-class), then that would seem to cancel out any claim that he's privileged in another.

But the truth is more complicated than whether *he* is privileged, because, as we saw earlier, privilege isn't really about him, even though he's certainly involved in it. The social categories "white," "male," and "middle-class," for example, are privileged in this society, and he belongs to two of those. Being working-class, however, can set up barriers that make it harder for him to attain the benefits associated with being white and male. If he can't earn a good living, for example, he may have a hard time feeling like a "real man" bonded to other men in their superiority to women. The privileged social category "male" still exists, and he belongs to it, but his social-class position gets in the way of his enjoying the unearned advantages that go with it.

Another complication is that categories that define privilege exist all at once and in relation to one another. People never see me solely in terms of my race, for example, or my gender. Like everyone else's place in the social world, mine is a package deal—white male nondisabled heterosexual (middle-aged, married, father, writer, teacher, middle-class, Anglo, U.S. citizen, and on and on)—and that's the way it is all the time.

Whether, for example, students perceive me as intelligent, credible, and competent will most likely be affected by their perception of my race. In that sense, no student could look at me simply as professor, because they also see a person of a certain gender, race, disability status, and class. Even if they first meet me on the phone, they form impressions of my race if only by assuming I'm white unless I give them reason to think otherwise. In this sense, I don't exist purely as a professor separate from the other social categories that I belong to.

Given that reality, it makes no sense to talk about the effect of being in one of these categories—say, white—without also looking at the others and how they're related to it. My experience of being identified as a white person in this society is affected by my also being seen as male, heterosexual, nondisabled, and of a certain class. If I apply for a job, for example, white privilege will usually give me an edge over a similarly qualified Latino. But if the people doing the hiring think I'm gay, my white privilege might lose out to his heterosexual privilege, and he might get the job instead of me.

It's tempting to use such comparisons to try to figure out some kind of net cost or benefit associated with each social category. In other words, you get a point for being white, male, heterosexual, or nondisabled, and you lose a point if you're of color, female, gay or lesbian, or have a disability. Add up the points and the result is your position in relation to privilege. That would put nondisabled white male heterosexuals on top (+4) and lesbians of color with disabilities in some kind of "quadruple jeopardy" at the bottom (–4). White nondisabled lesbians (0) and nondisabled gay men of color (0) would fall in between and presumably on the same "level."

Life and privilege aren't that simple, however. It's not as though being male gives you a certain amount of something called "privilege" and being white gives you more of the same, and being gay cancels out half of it. Privilege takes different forms that are connected to one another in ways that aren't obvious. For example, historically one of the ways that white men have justified their domination over black men has been to portray them as sexual predators who pose a threat to white women. At the same time, they've portrayed white women as pure and needing white men's protection, a dependent position that puts them under white men's control. Note, then, how the dynamics of gender and race are so bound up with each other that it's hard, if not impossible, to tell where one ends and the other begins. How much race or gender "counts" all by itself cannot be determined.

This is why sociologist Patricia Hill Collins describes such systems as a "matrix of domination" or why Estelle Disch calls them a "matrix of privilege"—and not merely a loose collection of different kinds of inequality that don't have much to do with one another. As Collins and numerous others argue, each particular form of privilege is part of a much larger system of privilege.[29]

Looking at privilege and domination in this way simplifies and clarifies things considerably. For example, once we see that each form of privilege exists in relation to all the rest, we can stop the fruitless habit of trying to figure out which is the worst or most oppressive.

We also free ourselves from the trap of thinking that everything is a matter of either/or—either you're oppressed or you're not, privileged or not—because reality is usually a matter of both/and. In other words, we can belong to both privileged and oppressed categories at the same time, and if we're going to make ourselves part of the solution to the problem of privilege, we have to see that. Why? Because we can't make ourselves part of the solution without seeing clearly how we're connected to the problem.

Perhaps most important, the concept of a matrix reveals how the different dimensions of privilege and domination are connected to one another. These connections happen in several ways. First, one form of privilege can defend or reinforce another. When women who challenge male privilege are called lesbians, for example, it tends to discredit them, which encourages women to remain silent regardless of their sexual orientation. In this way, the prejudice of heterosexism is used to support male privilege.

Second, access to one form of privilege can affect access to others. Because the advantages of race, for example, generally give white men greater access to class privilege compared with men of color, white men also have better access to male privilege. This happens in part because male privilege is increased by men earning more than their female partners, an advantage that is more difficult for men of color to achieve given their oppression because of race. In this way, white privilege has the effect of enhancing white men's access to male privilege. Note, however, that this works only for heterosexual white men, since being gay can seriously compromise a man's social standing as a "real man" and hence his access to male privilege.

Third, access to one form of privilege can serve as compensation for not having access to another. Men of color, for example, can make use of male privilege to compensate for their oppression under the weight of white privilege, just as white working-class men can use male privilege (and white privilege) to compensate for their lack of class privilege, or white women can use race privilege to compensate for the effects of gender oppression.

Finally, subordinate groups are often pitted against one another in ways that draw attention away from the system of privilege that hurts them all. Asian Americans, for example, are often held up as a good example—a "model minority." This makes other racial and ethnic minorities look bad by comparison and encourages them to blame Asian Americans for their disadvantaged status.[30] In this way, Asian Americans serve as a distraction and a buffer between whites and other peoples of color, as Korean Americans did in Los Angeles after the police who assaulted Rodney King were acquitted and the rage of black people spilled over into Korean neighborhoods, where stores were burned to the ground. Only when the rioting reached the edge of white neighborhoods did police finally respond to pleas for help.[31]

The complexity of the matrix of privilege and domination makes it clear that work for change needs to focus on the idea of privilege itself in all the forms it takes and how it conditions us to think of ourselves in relation to inequalities of power. We won't get rid of racism, in other words, without doing something about sexism and classism, because the system that produces the one also produces the others and connects them.

CHAPTER 4

Making Privilege Happen

Although privilege is attached to social categories and not to individuals, people are the ones who make it happen through what they do and don't do in relation to others. This almost always involves some form of discrimination—in other words, treating people unequally simply because they belong to a particular social category.[1] Whether it's done consciously or not, discrimination helps maintain systems of privilege. Giving admissions preference to the children of graduates from elite colleges and universities, for example, is an act of discrimination because it perpetuates elite privilege by favoring their children over others regardless of qualifications. In the same way, refusing to admit, say, Jewish students is discrimination because it perpetuates their oppressed position in relation to non-Jews.

Like all behavior, discrimination is connected to how we think and feel about people, and prejudice plays a powerful role in this.[2] Prejudice is a complicated thing, because it involves both ideas and feelings. Racial prejudice, for example, includes values that elevate whiteness above color and the belief that whites are smarter. It also includes negative feelings toward people of color—contempt, hostility, fear, disgust, and the like—along with positive (or at least neutral) feelings toward whites. Thus prejudice is a powerful force that provides fuel for discriminatory behavior and a rationale for justifying it.

Privilege, then, is something that happens through what people think and feel and do, and it takes many active forms, from overt hostility to the subtlety of looking away.[3] It works at every level, from the spirit and the body to having a decent place to live and enough food to eat. As sociologists Joe Feagin and Melvin Sikes point out in their book *Living with Racism,* the consequences of privilege must be understood as lived experience that both damages people in the moment and accumulates over time to affect not only their behavior but also their understanding of themselves and life itself.[4] And no matter what form privilege takes, it involves everyone in one way or another.

AVOIDANCE, EXCLUSION, REJECTION, AND WORSE

Of all human needs, few are as powerful as the need to be seen, included, and accepted by other people. This is why being shunned or banished is among the most painful punishments to endure, a social death. It's not surprising, then, that inclusion and acceptance are key aspects of privilege. To see how, consider all the choices people can make that affect whether other people feel welcome and valued or like outsiders who don't belong:

- Whether we look at people when we talk with them.
- Whether we smile at people when they come into the room, or stare as if to say, "What are *you* doing here?" or stop the conversation with a hush they have to wade through to be included in the smallest way.
- Whether we listen and respond to what people say, or drift away to someone or something else; whether we talk about things they know about, or stick to what's peculiar to the "in-group."
- Whether we acknowledge that diversity exists and make room for it, or act as though everyone is either like us or, by default, *should* be like us.

- Whether we acknowledge people's presence, or make them wait as if they weren't there; whether we avoid touching their skin when giving or taking something; how closely we watch them to see what they're up to.

- Whether we avoid someone going down the street, giving them a wide berth when we pass or even crossing to the other side.

- Whether we share with newcomers the informal rules that you have to know in order to succeed, belong, or get along—or turn the conversation to something light and superficial when they're around.

- Whether we invite people to our home or out to socialize.

- Whether we say hello to people when they move into the neighborhood.

Avoidance, exclusion, rejection, and devaluing often happen in ways noticed only by the person experiencing them, and they can happen without anyone intending harm. It can be as subtle as shifting your gaze, leaning your body away, or editing your speech. It can be faint praise ("Uh-huh, okay"), or praise that's so effusive ("Wow, you're really articulate!"), it signals surprise at the person's having exceeded low expectations. It can be repeatedly asking someone if they understand what you've said, as if they're too stupid to have gotten it the first time. It can be using images of darkness and blackness as negative, and light and whiteness as positive, or using "queer" or "gay" as insults, or "having balls" (but not ovaries) as a metaphor for courage. It can be paying more attention to a woman's looks than to her ability or character, and encouraging her to do the same. It can be as unmindful as assuming that all people are Christian ("Merry Christmas!") or heterosexual ("Feel free to bring your husband/wife.") or able to climb a flight of stairs. It can be as simple as not paying attention, as when elegantly dressed black presidential candidate Jesse Jackson was tipped by a white woman who confused him with a bellman who'd just helped her in a New York hotel.[5] It can be telling what seems to be a joke but in fact signals the low esteem in which people are held simply because they're female or gay or disabled or of color.

To look at racism in particular, as subtle as it often is, racism also happens openly and on purpose. It appears in swastikas and racial epithets scrawled on college dormitory walls, in Asian American students receiving hate mail or being spat on as they walk across campus. It appears in crosses burned on front lawns of African Americans who've just moved into a neighborhood, and in churches and synagogues burned to the ground and graveyards strewn with toppled tombstones.

It happens when real estate agents steer people of color away from white neighborhoods and bank officers deny them mortgages and business loans readily granted to whites who are no more qualified than they are, making blacks the most residentially segregated group in the United States. The consequences of this inequity are almost incalculable, for study after study shows that geographic mobility is a key to social mobility and improved quality of life. Where people live makes a huge difference in the jobs they have access to, the quality of community services (schools, health care, street maintenance, trash disposal), and their ability to affect those who govern them.[6]

Racism comes out in police harassment, brutality, and neglect in moments of crisis or in being pulled over and having your car searched for a "DWB" ("Driving While Black") violation. It comes out in black parents' having to train their teenage sons to avoid the police at all costs, to never run away if they do encounter them, to keep their hands out in the open, to never give cause for suspicion—in other words, to never act like a child moving through the world freely and without fear. It comes out in "nigger" muttered in passing on a crowded sidewalk or scrawled on public bathroom walls, and in billboard advertising campaigns for cigarettes and alcohol that target lower- and working-class African American neighborhoods. It comes out in vacant apartments that suddenly become unavailable, in hotel reservations mysteriously "lost" when a person of color arrives to claim them.

For African Americans, the result is a daily grind of always feeling vulnerable to judgments based solely on their race, because mistakes and failure are never just that but always carry the potential to "confirm the broader, racial inferiority they are suspected of."[7] Racism means living in a society that predisposes whites to see the worst in people of color and ignore the best, a society in which acceptance must be won anew every day. It means having to carry a continuing "minority sense," a "race watch" for the possibility of hostility, and a "second eye" to decide whether to give whites the benefit of the doubt.[8]

"It is utterly exhausting being Black in America," writes children's advocate Marian Wright Edelman, who is black. "Physically, mentally, and emotionally. . . . There is no respite from your badge of color."[9]

It is, as a black college professor put it, to lead "lives of quiet desperation generated by a litany of *daily* large and small events that, whether or not by design, remind us of our 'place' in American society."[10] It is to experience a precarious balance between paranoia and the desire to live life simply as it comes, an endless struggle with humiliation, depression, and rage.

Racism, of course, isn't the only form of exclusion and oppression. An ongoing epidemic of violence threatens women and gay men, for example, at home and at work and on the street. A majority of girls and women in U.S. schools and workplaces report being sexually harassed, domestic violence is a leading cause of injury to women, and almost half of all females born in the United States can expect to experience an attempted or completed rape sometime during their lives.[11] The result is patterns of chronic fear and avoidance as women and girls learn to circumscribe their lives in order to reduce the odds of being singled out for harassment or attack.

When subordinate groups get fed up and express rage, frustration, and resentment, there's always the danger that powerful others—men, whites, Anglos, the nondisabled, heterosexuals, the middle and upper classes—won't like it and will retaliate with the epithets "unprofessional," "malcontent," "maladjusted," "whiner," "too emotional," "bitch," "out of control," or "male-basher."[12] Given the cultural authority and power to harm that such retaliation carries, there isn't a lot that people can do to defend themselves against it.

The problem of privilege infects both our outer and inner lives and flows between them in ways that intensify and perpetuate both. It appears in unequal distributions of income and wealth that grow worse as competition intensifies over jobs that pay a living wage and as the concentration of wealth and power in corporations and the upper classes expands in the global economy. It appears in unequal treatment, access, and opportunities in education, work, health care, and the courts and in severe underrepresentation in every major organization from religious to corporate to political.

At work, the effects of privilege show up in glass ceilings and occupational ghettos. Asian Americans, for example, are routinely treated like "techno-coolies" to be managed for their talents but never allowed to manage themselves or others,[13] and to be channeled into narrow technical specialties and then envied and resented when they excel at them.

Jobs are so segregated by gender that half of all workers would have to change occupations in order for women and men to be equally represented across the U.S. economy. The dynamics of privilege are also reflected in upper-level jobs such as "community relations" that for all their apparent trappings of success are often dead-end pedestals for displaying—and containing—minority tokens. Or in the positions of white women and people of color who don't get mentored and whose potential and accomplishments are all but invisible. Blacks and Latinas/Latinos, for example, are significantly underrepresented in managerial and professional occupations, often averaging only a half to two-thirds of their proportional share of the employed labor force. They are significantly *over*represented in clerical and support occupations, government jobs such as mail carriers, and lower-level service and blue-collar jobs.[14]

And while education certainly helps, in many ways it doesn't help much. African Americans and Latinas/Latinos with four or more years of college are, respectively, 83 and 61 percent more likely to be unemployed than comparable whites. African American and Latina/Latino families with college-educated householders are two to three times more likely than similar white families to live below the poverty line.[15] Similar dynamics work in regard to gender inequality. Although the gender gap in income has shrunk somewhat over the long haul, the pace is extremely slow and over the last few decades has been as likely to go down as up. In 1982, women college graduates who worked full time and year-round earned an average of $17,000 compared with $28,000 for men, a ratio of 62 cents to the dollar. By 2000, the comparable averages had risen to $47,224 for women and $77,963 for men, a ratio of only 61 cents to the dollar.[16]

Among people with disabilities, the unemployment rate is 12 times higher than it is for people without disabilities, in spite of the fact that the vast majority of unemployed people with disabilities want to work. People with disabilities are also three times more likely to live in households with incomes of $15,000 or less, in part because many of those who work must accept jobs that pay less than the minimum wage.[17] Many of these jobs lack benefits such as health insurance, and, as a result, people with disabilities are more than twice as likely as those without disabilities to postpone needed health care because they cannot afford it.[18]

In all its forms, the problem of privilege and oppression stands between us and the kind of world in which all people have the best chance of thriving. To do something about this problem, we first have to see how it affects us, because only then are we likely to feel a personal obligation to work for something better.

A PROBLEM FOR WHOM?

No matter where we look—and for all the complaints and controversy about affirmative action—the position of dominant groups shows little sign of weakening. However, the people who belong to them don't escape the negative consequences of privilege. Consider, for example, the impoverishment of men's lives caused by the culturally encouraged emotional gulfs between them and their fathers, sons, and male friends. Consider the damage men often do to themselves and one another in trying to measure up as "real men," how they limit their humanity, deny their needs, don't ask for help, and often live with chronic fear, anxiety, isolation, and loneliness. Consider men's fear of other men's violence and aggression, and boys who feel driven to shoot down classmates and teachers. Consider the difficulty of true cross-gender friendship and of men's predictable defensiveness around women—men feel vulnerable to accusations of sexism or harassment in a world organized to privilege them at women's expense. Consider the range of reactions to the most subtle mention of male privilege: hypersensitive, huffy, hurt, worried, hostile, confused, shut down, tuned out, unable to "get it," rushing to backpedal, dismiss, counter, refute, condescend, patronize, trivialize, ridicule, or just walk away.

The disadvantages of male privilege are similar to those of heterosexual privilege. By definition, gay men and lesbians bear the brunt of heterosexism and homophobia.[19] But the dynamic that harms them also has destructive effects on heterosexuals. In the simplest sense, weapons used against gays and lesbians are also used among heterosexuals, especially among men. Power plays a key role in gender dynamics, especially in patterns of gender inequality. But it also looms large in men's competition with other men—the jockeying for status and trying to measure up to mainstream standards of masculinity. As part of this dynamic, the same insults and intimidation that heterosexual men use against gay men—"fag," "queer," "fairy," "cocksucker"—they also routinely use against other heterosexual men to enhance their status. Sometimes such tags are used openly, but the message is often coded in words such as "wimp," "wuss," or "whipped." In either case, whenever a man's manhood is challenged, his vulnerability to being tarred with cultural references to being gay is never far off, regardless of whether his sexual orientation is truly in doubt. As we saw earlier, similar dynamics operate to intimidate women into silence on the subject of male privilege for fear of being tagged as lesbians.[20]

This particular gender dynamic among men gives only a hint of the trouble heterosexuals are in. Consider the enormous amount of male aggression, violence, and harassment directed at girls and women, from child sexual abuse to battering, rape, and sexual harassment.[21] Studies of male violence show that control is a core issue, especially through the cultural connection between power ("potency") and heterosexual relationships. A real man is defined as one who is always in control, and sexuality is identified as a major way for men to prove it. Since violence is primarily a means for exerting control and asserting superiority, the cultural association between heterosexuality and male power actually promotes male violence against women in heterosexual relationships.

Because heterosexuality plays such a large part in defining gender inequality—"real" men and women are always defined in heterosexual terms—gender violence often has a sexual aspect to it. As a result, the violence inflicted on lesbians and gay men by heterosexual men and the violence among heterosexual couples are deeply related to each other.[22]

Most heterosexual men who attack lesbians and gay men do so not because of moral or religious conviction but because they feel threatened and uneasy over the mere existence of people whose sexual orientation and relation to women raise questions about their own. Since lesbians and gay men don't follow heterosexual models, the example they set challenges heterosexual men's claim to a monopoly over "real manhood," especially as measured by power over women. The example set by gay men also challenges the dominant masculine model by their not relating to women as objects of sexual power. Lesbians challenge it by not choosing or submitting to men as sexual partners. This makes it hard to separate the dynamics of gender inequality in heterosexual relationships and the trouble heterosexuals make for gays and lesbians.

Just as there is gender trouble for men and heterosexist trouble for heterosexuals, there is also race trouble for whites. It shows up in all the things white people do to get around the fact that the enormous suffering caused by racism has something to do with the social status of being white, no matter how whites see themselves as individuals.[23] It is reflected in discomfort and fear around blacks, in demonizing black men and boys, in hypersensitive defensiveness around issues of race.[24] You can see the race trouble for whites in the uneasy feeling they often get when they realize they aren't trusted and are being told what they want to hear rather than the truth. You can see it in how white people deaden themselves against the pain they'd feel if they realized how deeply racism compromises their own lives, how much it deadens the spirit and flattens the emotional landscape, how it sets whites up to look at the "rhythm" and "life" in non-European cultures with the nagging feeling of something lacking in their own.

You can see the race trouble for whites in the toll it takes on moral integrity, because racism requires hypocrisy toward deeply held cultural values of fairness, decency, and justice. You can see it in the lengths to which white people will often go to distort current and historical reality to maintain the illusion of being the chosen and superior race, the standard against which others are to be measured. You can see it in how poorly prepared white people are to be effective on a global scale, where whites are, for all their power, a small and shrinking minority. You can see it in the angry, wishful naïveté of

"I don't see color. I don't see race." You can see it in the pointed ignoring of the "deceptively comfortable prison" of racism that white people live in and the chronic fear that "the murky waters of despair and dread that now flood the streets of black America" will touch them, too, if not sweep them and everything they cherish away.[25]

But the trouble of race already touches them. White people are up to their necks in it just by being here.

What we don't realize most of the time is that the "isms"—sexism, heterosexism, ableism, racism—affect more than women, gays or lesbians, people with disabilities, and people of color. They affect everyone, because it's impossible to live in a world that generates so much injustice and suffering without being touched by it. Everyone has a race, a gender, a sexual orientation, a disability status. Whether we like it or not, we all figure in the differences that privilege and oppression are about. The bad news is that no matter who you are, the trouble is *your* trouble. But that's also the good news, because it gives you a reason to do something about it.

AND THAT'S NOT ALL

In addition to how it affects people, the trouble that surrounds privilege also affects organizations, communities, and society as a whole. In corporations and the military and neighborhood schools, the prevalence of privilege and oppression is among our worst-kept secrets. Much of the time, people manage to act as though nothing's wrong—and then another scandal explodes onto the front pages: racist talk and behavior at the highest levels of responsibility and power; Matthew Shepard, a young man tortured and murdered in 1998 because of his sexual orientation; sexual violence and harassment allowed to go on at the U.S. Air Force Academy and at companies as prominent as Ford Motor Company; hate crimes in the halls of colleges and universities, institutions that present themselves as sanctuaries for enlightenment and reason.

Most organizations either deny the trouble or are oblivious to it. When a crisis breaks through the routine of business as usual, the typical reaction is panicked efforts at damage control to minimize legal exposure and bad publicity. Invariably, the attention goes to a few misbehaving individuals, in the belief that getting rid of or fixing them or learning how to spot them before they do something wrong is enough to take care of the problem.

Between crises and scandals, privilege continues its insidious work of making organizations increasingly dysfunctional and vulnerable. It makes it all but impossible, for example, for white male managers and teachers to effectively mentor white women and people of color—if they even try in the first place, which they usually don't. White men's position in the world gives them few ways to know what their female and minority students and junior colleagues are up against as they try to move upward in organizations. White men also see little reason to examine themselves in relation to the racism and sexism that haunt so many people's lives, to come to terms with how living in a racist and sexist world has shaped them and how they see other people and themselves. They might try to be fair, which is to say, to treat people of color as they would whites, or women as they would men. But this approach pretends that racism and sexism don't exist beyond their personal intentions, and it makes it easier for them to feel unconnected to the trouble. It also doesn't serve the needs of people on the outside looking in.

If the teacher or the boss won't talk about privilege and oppression, the subordinate trying to learn the ropes and get ahead is unlikely to take the risk of making powerful people uncomfortable by bringing them up. With so much of importance left unsaid and such crucial issues left untouched, it's hard to trust those in power—and, on some level, there's good reason not to. As a result, people don't learn what they need to know to succeed. They wind up stuck in place, or in some backwater position within the organization, their talents and abilities unrealized and of no particular use to anyone, including themselves. Or they strike out on their own, dropping out of school or transferring to another university, for example, or leaving a job to start their own business or to work for a company that understands the importance of meeting the issue head-on.

For the organizations that are left behind, their investment in training and development is lost, and the word goes out that if you aren't white, aren't heterosexual, aren't nondisabled, aren't male, and aren't desperate, you'll do better someplace else, someplace where you can look at those with power and influence and see people who look like you. And as competition intensifies and the population of students and workers diversifies, those "someplace elses" wind up doing better because they attract and keep talent that comes in all kinds of people.

Most organizations' failure in the area of diversity occurs not because they're run by mean-spirited bigots—few are—but because they deal with issues of privilege badly or not at all, unless a crisis forces the issue. Even then, they deal with it only enough to make it *seem* to go away, which usually doesn't include confronting the reality of privilege and oppression.

The failure doesn't happen all at once in some dramatic moment of truth. The splashy scandals—the inflammatory incident, the raving bigot found out, the harassing professor unmasked—aren't the problem. The problem is the same culture of denial and neglect that permeates society as a whole. Little by little, day by day, the struggle to earn a living or a degree and maintain a sense of dignity and self-worth in the face of one sign after another that they don't really matter or belong wears people down, sapping morale and draining talent.

The oppressive effect of privilege is often so insidious that dominant groups complain whenever it's brought up for discussion. They feel impatient and imposed on. "Come on," they say, "stop whining. Things aren't that bad. Maybe they used to be, but not anymore. It's time to move on. Get over it." But people who are white or heterosexual or male or nondisabled or middle- or upper-class have to ask themselves how they would *know* how bad it really is to be a person of color or a lesbian or a woman or gay or disabled or working- or lower-class. What life experience, for example, would qualify a white person to know the day-to-day reality of racism? People of color are, by comparison, experts in the dynamics of race privilege, because they live with the oppressive consequences of it twenty-four hours a day. White people simply do not. Whites may know what it's like to get bad service in a restaurant, for example, but they have no idea what it's like to get bad service so often—and to have it happen to all their friends and relations—that they can't escape the reality that it's tied to how people see them as human beings simply because of their race.[26]

None of this means that everything said by people in subordinate groups is true. But it does mean that there's every reason for members of dominant groups to give them the benefit of the doubt long enough to look at what they're talking about.

WE CAN'T HEAL UNTIL
THE WOUNDING STOPS

There is a lot of talk these days about "racial healing," healing "gender wounds," and "reconciliation" of various kinds. These are powerful and inspiring images that carry the promise of a soothing end to a difficult and destructive time in U.S. history. The war is over, the damage done. Now we can turn to the difficult but ultimately triumphant work of undoing the damage and healing the wounds inflicted individually and collectively.

If true, this solution would be a blessing, but in fact it represents wishful thinking, because problems of privilege and oppression are far from over. Every day they damage tens of millions of people. The patterns of history continue into the present and show every sign of going on into the future unless people do something to change them. And the only way to do that is to change the role these patterns play in making privilege happen.

Healing imagery is also problematic because it implies that the damage being done is primarily emotional. The goal becomes one of "getting along" better by being nicer and more tolerant toward one another, forgiving and forgetting, living in more authentic ways. I don't object to this goal, but it ignores the fact that a lot of the trouble doesn't begin and end with interpersonal relations and emotional wounds. Much of it is embedded in structures of power and inequality that shape almost every aspect of life in this society, from economics to politics to religion to schools and the family. The idea that we're going to get out of this by somehow getting to a place where we're kinder and more sensitive to one another ignores most of what we have to overcome. It sets us up to walk right past the trouble toward an alternative that doesn't exist and can't exist until we do something about what creates privilege and oppression in the first place. And that is something that needs to be changed, not healed.

In some ways, appeals to healing turn out to be—in effect if not intent—another way to deny the depth of the trouble we're in. They feed on the desperate and powerful illusion that if we ignore it long enough, or try to replace it with good intentions, it will go away. But the hope for something better depends on the ability to work together to face that illusion and go through it to the truth on the other side. To do that, we first have to understand how the trouble that surrounds privilege is made worse by how we think about it—the trouble we have with the trouble.

CHAPTER 5

The Trouble with the Trouble

I am in a three-day meeting of human resource managers. It is one of the most diverse groups I've ever seen—roughly half women and half men, half white and half people of color, and from all over the United States as well as a dozen European countries. These people share a deep and in many cases lifelong commitment to ending privilege and oppression and are responsible for some of the best success stories large organizations have to tell.

As I listen to them talk about their work, it's obvious how frustrated they are in spite of all they've accomplished. Progress is painfully slow and easily undone when leadership changes or a budget crunch dries up resources needed to carry the work forward. But the malaise goes deeper, to the horns of a dilemma that emerges as the day wears on. They know that the only way to deal effectively with these issues is to engage managers and vice presidents who have the power to shape organizational culture and set examples that bring others along. They also know that "manager" or "vice president" usually means "white heterosexual nondisabled male," because that's who the overwhelming majority of people in control of large organizations are, whether it's universities, unions, government, churches, professional sports, or the mass media.

Everyone in the room knows that the key is to engage members of dominant groups with issues of privilege as an ongoing, permanent part of their lives. Privilege has to be as much an issue for them as it is for those who bear the brunt of the oppression it causes in everyday life.

In other words, if dominant groups *really* saw privilege and oppression as unacceptable—if white people saw race as *their* issue, if nondisabled people saw ableism as *their* problem—privilege and oppression wouldn't have much of a future. But this isn't what's happening. Dominant groups *don't* engage with these issues, and when they do, it's not for long or with much effect.

I ask the human resource managers "Why not?" and the response pours out of them without hesitation. Dominant groups don't see privilege as a problem

- *Because they don't know it exists in the first place.* They're oblivious to it. The reality of privilege doesn't occur to them because they don't go out of their way to see it or ask about it and because no one dares bring it up for fear of making things worse. Dominant groups have no idea of how their privilege oppresses others. This obliviousness allows them to cruise along and tend to the details of their own lives (which are, of course, considerable, just like everyone else's), with only an occasional sense of trouble somewhere "out there" just beyond the fringe of their consciousness. This lack of awareness also gives them a low tolerance for hearing about the trouble: when the normal state of affairs is silence, any mention of it feels like an imposition.[1]

- *Because they don't have to.* If you point it out to them, they may acknowledge that the trouble exists. Otherwise, they don't pay attention, because privilege insulates them from its consequences. There is nothing to compel their attention except, perhaps, when a schoolyard shooting or a sexual harassment lawsuit or a race riot disrupts the usual flow of things.

- *Because they think it's just a personal problem.* They think individuals usually get what they deserve, which makes the trouble just a sum of individual troubles. This means that if whites or males get more than others, it's because they have it coming—they work harder, they're smarter, more capable. If other people get less, it's up to them to do something about it.

■ *Because they want to hang on to their privilege.* On some level, they know that they benefit from the status quo and that they don't want that to change. Some people have mixed feelings, such as a white man who said in a workshop that he felt "torn between wanting to make things right and not wanting to lose what I have." Many others, however, feel a sense of entitlement, that they deserve everything they have, including whatever advantages they have over others. As one male student at a university in Colorado said to me, "Why should men's athletic programs have to give up any funding to women? If they want more money for their programs, let them go find it." Such feelings can be especially powerful among those whose lack of class privilege leads them to deny the very existence of other forms of privilege they have. For them, resistance to change isn't about hanging on to privilege, because they don't experience themselves as having any. Instead, they see themselves as struggling to succeed in a system that is based on competition and scarcity and are reluctant to lose anything that gives them an edge. Similar dynamics sometimes appear among those who are privileged by their class position. I once worked with a group of highly successful white professional women, for example, who became furious when we pressed them on issues of race. They were happy to talk about male privilege and how it frustrated their upward mobility but wanted no part of the idea that privilege attached to their own whiteness was something they needed to look at.

■ *Because they're prejudiced—racist, sexist, heterosexist, ableist, classist.* They're consciously hostile toward blacks, women, lesbians, gay men, people with disabilities or in poverty. They believe in the superiority of their group, and the belief is like a thick wall. The more you try to get through it or over it, the higher and thicker it gets. They're the white executives who talk in racist ways in the privacy of their offices, the Army drill sergeants who sexually assault female trainees, the professors who harass female students by pressuring them for sex or holding them

up for ridicule in their classes, the middle-class people who
look the other way when they pass a homeless person on the
street, or a presidential candidate who vows not to appoint gay
or lesbian Cabinet secretaries.

- *Because they're afraid.* They may be sympathetic to doing something about privilege and oppression, but they're afraid of
  being blamed if they acknowledge that it exists. They're afraid
  of being saddled with guilt just for being white or male or
  nondisabled or middle-class, attacked with no place to hide.
  They're even more afraid that members of their own group—
  other whites, other heterosexuals, other men—will reject them
  if they break ranks and call attention to issues of privilege,
  making people feel uncomfortable or threatened. Since even
  these beneficiaries of privilege are often worried and frightened already about so many things in their lives—such as
  losing their jobs or being passed over for promotion—this
  challenge appears as just one more thing to be afraid of.

These reasons don't apply to everyone in the same way or to the
same degree, in part because "they" aren't a homogeneous group of
people. As we've seen, privilege is complicated, and each of its various dimensions, such as gender or disability status, affects how people
deal with its other dimensions.

Regardless of such variations and exceptions, if members of dominant groups pay attention to privilege and oppression, it's always in
spite of the many reasons not to. Dealing with those reasons brings us
to the core dilemma of diversity.

The roomful of human resource managers were responsible for
success stories in raising consciousness in organizations. Why, then,
were they so frustrated and so painfully aware of things *not* working
for change? As I listened to them, I realized that the progress they
had made depended on two strategies that are effective, but to a limited degree and, even then, only in the short run. Because the managers saw these strategies as their only alternatives, they felt stuck.
And they are.

The first strategy is to appeal to privileged people's sense of
decency and fairness, their good will toward those less fortunate than
themselves, what one manager calls the "tin cup" approach. "Help us

do something about these issues," the pitch goes, "because it's a good and noble thing to do."

The tin cup approach touches many people and sometimes even moves them to action, but as a strategy for long-term change it fails for several reasons. It depends on an impulse of generosity toward others, and this impulse tends to rise and fall depending on how secure the privileged feel in their own situations. This is why even the most progressive organizations will support diversity work when their bottom line is healthy and cut back at the first sign of hard times (in the same way that public schools cut back on art, music, and other "expressive" programs when money gets tight).

The do-a-good-deed approach also rests on a sense of "us" and "them"—the "us" who help and the less fortunate "them" who get helped. The problem is that the former feel very little reason to identify with the latter. When "we" who are not poor or with disabilities, for example, help out "those people" who are poor or with disabilities, there can be a real separation and distance even at the moment of reaching out to help. In fact, the act of helping—of being able to help—can reaffirm the social distance between the two groups and heighten everyone's awareness of it. Thus every such act of giving to others is always a statement, intended or not, of one group's ability to give and the other's inability to get along without it. And in a society that counts independence, autonomy, and self-sufficiency among its highest cultural values, it's impossible to avoid the negative judgments attached to those on the receiving end and the status-enhancing judgments conferred on those who give.

Although doing the right thing can be morally compelling, it usually rests on a sense of obligation to principle more than to people, which can lead to disconnection rather than connection. I take care of my children, for example, not because it's the right thing to do and the neighbors would disapprove if I didn't, but because I feel a sense of connection to them that carries with it an automatic sense of responsibility for their welfare. The less connected to them I feel, the less responsible I'll feel. It isn't that I *owe* them something as a debtor owes a creditor. It's rather that my life is bound up in their lives and theirs in mine, which means that what happens to them in a sense also happens to me. I don't experience them as "others" whom

I decide to help because I'm feeling charitable at the moment. The family is something larger than myself that I participate in, and I can't be part of that without paying attention to what goes on in it.

Another problem with acting merely from a sense of principle is that part of its appeal is the good feeling it gives people about themselves when they do it, which can motivate them only in the short run. Confronting issues such as sexism and racism is hard and sometimes painful and even frightening work, and feeling good about being virtuous isn't likely to sustain people over the rugged course of it.

What can sustain them is a sense of *ownership*, that the trouble is truly *their* trouble and not someone else's, because this means their responsibility to do something no longer feels like an option. It isn't something they can choose to do if they're in a generous mood or can "afford" to at the moment. It is, quite simply, one of the terms of their participation in the world they live in, however large or small they define it to be. Without that sense of ownership, serious work on issues of privilege will always be what Roosevelt Thomas calls a "fair weather" item on the agenda.[2]

Thomas urges us to follow an alternative to the tin cup approach. We should do something about privilege and oppression, he tells us, not because it's the socially responsible, right thing to do but because it makes organizations work better. It helps businesses compete for customers and the best employees and universities compete for the best students, faculty, and staff. It raises morale and productivity and lowers costly turnovers. It protects against lawsuits and all the energy that goes into worrying about them.

In an important sense, of course, he's right. For corporations and universities, the "business case" for dealing with the trouble around privilege is a compelling one. It underlies the most successful corporate initiatives at companies like Dow Corning and Avon. When women and racial minorities leave unsupportive workplaces and take their training and talent with them, the annual loss to organizations can run into millions of dollars. That's far more than it would cost to fund programs to improve the conditions that prompt people to leave. When you factor in the other costs and liabilities that result from an unsupportive or hostile environment, you'd think organizations would fall all over themselves in the rush to do something about it.

But most of the time they don't, and when they do, it often comes across as a halfhearted, short-lived, "flavor of the month" program that can leave people feeling cynical and, having had their expectations raised and dashed, even worse than before. ("It pisses me off," said a woman line supervisor at one of the largest U.S. manufacturers, "that they're doing this just to make a buck.") Or the program is serious and intense but lacks follow-up or fades away when key people leave or budgets are cut or companies merge. The problem with relying on the business case is that it sees ending the trouble as a means to an end, a practical, rational strategy. Thus it's only as good as the results it produces in comparison with alternative strategies. If a more "efficient" way can be found to improve the bottom line or protect against losses—especially in the short run—then it's likely to replace the diversity strategy.

This is why the business case, for all its surface validity, cannot be the *only* basis for action. At the right moment, the business case can appeal to fear or greed or both, but as anyone knows who watches the ups and downs of the stock market, fear is something that comes and goes, and greed easily attaches itself to whatever looks good at the moment. This is especially true in the short run, which is increasingly the perspective of choice in a competitive and insecure global capitalist economy.

Short-run thinking encourages organizations to act like Hindus in India who make the mistake of eating their cows during droughts when food is in short supply. Cows are vital to Indian agriculture. They serve as draft animals in rice fields (their cloven hooves don't get stuck in the muck), and their dung is used for everything from building blocks to fuel. In the middle of a famine, a cow can look awfully good as a short-run solution to hunger. But giving in to the temptation leads to long-run disaster, because when the rains return, you can't raise any crops because you've eaten your most important farming resource. Anthropologist Marvin Harris argues that this is why the cow became a sacred symbol in the Hindu religion—it was the only way powerful enough to keep people from eating their cows when the temptation was the greatest.[3]

Organizations that ignore issues of privilege and oppression are in effect eating their cows by focusing only on short-run consequences. When push comes to shove and they need all the talent and commitment they can get in a highly competitive world, it simply won't be there. The human potential that comes in packages that don't qualify as white or male or heterosexual or nondisabled will be long gone, fled across the street to competitors willing to confront these issues and do something about them.

Certainly life would be better in a world without privilege and oppression. Surely removing the resentment, fear, injustice, and suffering that go with them would dramatically improve life in schools, workplaces, neighborhoods, and communities. Short-run competitive thinking, however, makes that goal all but impossible to achieve, because effecting that kind of change is inherently a long-term project. Even when people can see the benefits somewhere off in the distance, they still need something to hold them to the vision and see them through the long journey from here to there. Appealing to lofty principles or the bottom line can't do it, because those approaches too easily give way to forces and considerations that are powerful in the short run even if they're disastrous in the long run.

What's needed is a sense of ownership in relation to the problem and the path people need to walk toward its solution. What's needed is some reason to feel committed to change that's powerful enough to win out against all the reasons dominant groups have to turn away and leave the problem to someone else—all the anger, fear, resentment, detachment, inattention, and ignorance, all wrapped up in the luxury of obliviousness. The personal stake in issues of privilege runs deeper than that, to the realization that everyone is connected to a great deal of suffering in the world, and anyone who allows awareness of that to enter their consciousness is bound to feel something about it.

We need a third choice, one that can take us beyond simple appeals to goodness or enhancing the bottom line. We need a way to remove the barriers that keep well-intentioned members of dominant groups stuck in a place where they don't see themselves as part of the solution. We need ways to have serious conversations across difference and to *act* across difference toward ending the most damaging source of unnecessary suffering in the human experience.

But to find them, we have to begin with what most people don't want to look at, which is what privilege, power, and difference have to do with us.

CHAPTER 6

What It All Has to Do with Us

To do something about the trouble surrounding privilege, power, and difference, we have to talk about it, but most of the time we don't, because it feels too risky. This is true for just about everyone, but especially for people with privilege. As Paul Kivel writes, for example, "Rarely do we whites sit back and listen to people of color without interrupting, without being defensive, without trying to regain attention to ourselves, without criticizing or judging."[1]

The discomfort, defensiveness, and fear come in part from not knowing how to talk about privilege without feeling vulnerable to anger and blame. Those feelings will hold us back until we find a way to reduce the risk of talking about privilege. The key to that lies in understanding what makes talking about privilege *seem* so risky. I don't mean that risk is an illusion. There is no way to do this work without the possibility that people will feel uncomfortable or frightened or threatened. But the risk isn't nearly as big as it seems, because, like the proverbial (and mythical) human fear of the strange and unfamiliar, the problem begins with how people *think* about things and who they are in relation to them.

INDIVIDUALISM: OR, THE MYTH THAT
EVERYTHING IS SOMEBODY'S FAULT

We live in a society that encourages us to think that the social world begins and ends with individuals. It's as if an organization or a society is just a collection of people, and everything that happens in it begins with what each person thinks, feels, and intends. If you understand people, the reasoning goes, then you also understand social life. It's an appealing way to think, because it's grounded in our experience as individuals, which is what we know best. But it's also misleading, because it boxes us into a narrow and distorted view of reality. In other words, it isn't true.

If we use individualism to explain sexism, for example, it's hard to avoid the idea that sexism exists simply because men *are* sexist—men have sexist feelings, beliefs, needs, and motivations that lead them to behave in sexist ways. If sexism produces evil consequences, it's because men *are* evil, hostile, and malevolent toward women. In short, everything bad in the world is seen as somebody's fault, which is why talk about privilege so often turns into a game of hot potato.

Individualistic thinking keeps us stuck in the trouble by making it so hard to talk about it. It encourages women, for example, to blame and distrust men. It sets men up to feel personally attacked if anyone mentions gender issues and to define those issues as a "women's problem." It also encourages men who don't think or behave in overtly sexist ways—the ones most likely to become part of the solution—to conclude that sexism has nothing to do with them, that it's just a problem for "bad" men. If well-intentioned men don't include themselves in the problem, they are unlikely to feel compelled to include themselves in the solution.

Individualistic thinking also makes us blind to the very existence of privilege, because privilege, by definition, has nothing to do with individuals, only with the social categories we wind up in. Individualistic thinking, however, assumes that everything has *only* to do with individuals and *nothing* to do with social categories, leaving no room to see, much less consider, the role of privilege.

The result of individualistic thinking is a kind of paralysis. Either people talk about sexism in the most superficial, unthreatening, trivializing, and even silly way ("The Battle of the Sexes," *Men Are from Mars, Women Are from Venus*) or they don't talk about it at all.[2]

Breaking the paralysis begins with realizing that the individualistic model is wrong, that the social world consists of a lot more than individuals. We are always participating in something larger than ourselves—what sociologists call *social systems*—and systems are not collections of people. A university, for example, is a social system, and people participate in it. But the people aren't the university, and the university isn't the people. This means that to understand what happens in it, we have to look at both the university and how individual people participate in it. If patterns of male privilege exist in a society, for example, the reason is never just a matter of men's personalities, feelings, or intentions. We also have to understand how they participate in particular kinds of social systems, how this participation shapes their behavior, and the consequences it produces.

INDIVIDUALS, SYSTEMS, AND PATHS OF LEAST RESISTANCE

Contrary to the individualistic model, social life happens only as people participate in social systems—families, schools, workplaces, religious organizations, and so on. If we want to understand what happens in the world, including patterns of privilege and oppression, we have to understand the dynamic relation between people and social systems.

As Figure 2 shows, the relationship between systems and individuals has two parts. The arrow on the right side represents the idea that as we participate in social systems, we are shaped as individual people in two ways. The first is the process of socialization through which we learn to participate in social life. From families, schools, religion, and the mass media, through the examples set by parents, peers, coaches, teachers, and public figures—in short, from just about every direction we are exposed to ideas and images of the world and who we are in relation to it and other people. We learn to name things and people, to value one thing or kind of person above another, to distinguish what's considered "normal" and acceptable from what is not.

Through all this, we develop a sense of personal identity—including gender, race, ethnicity, class, religion, disability status, and

FIGURE 2. Individuals and Systems.

sexual orientation—and of how that identity positions us in relation to other people, especially in terms of inequalities of power. As I grew up watching movies and television, for example, the message came through loud and clear that straight white men are the most important people on the planet because they're the ones who supposedly do the most important things. They're the strong ones who build; the heroes who fight the good fight; the geniuses, writers, and artists who create; the bold leaders who govern; and even the evil—but always interesting—villains. Even God is gendered male and raced as white, just like me (but, in terms of gender, not my mother or my sister).

Among the many consequences of all these messages is to encourage dominant groups to feel a sense of entitlement in relation to subordinate groups. Men, for example, are encouraged to expect women to tend and take care of them, to defer to and support men no matter how badly men behave. In the typical episode of the television sitcom *Everybody Loves Raymond,* for example, Ray Barone routinely behaves toward his wife, Debra, in ways that are insensitive, sexist, adolescent, and downright stupid, but by the end of each half hour we always find out why she puts up with it year after year—for some reason that's never made clear, she just loves the guy. This sends the message that it's reasonable for a heterosexual man to expect to "have" an intelligent and beautiful woman who will love him and stay with him in spite of his behaving badly toward her a great deal of the time.

Invariably, some of what we learn through socialization turns out not to be true and then we may have to deal with that. I say "may" because powerful forces encourage us to keep ourselves in a state of denial, to rationalize what we've learned in order to keep it safe from scrutiny, if only to protect our sense of who we are and ensure our being accepted by other people, including parents and family and friends. In the end, the default position is to adopt the dominant version of reality and act as though it's the only one there is.

The second way we are shaped as individuals by participating in social systems is through what I call "paths of least resistance."

In every social situation, we have an almost limitless number of choices we might make. Sitting in a movie theater, for example, we could go to sleep, sing, eat dinner, undress, dance, take out a flashlight and read the newspaper, carry on loud conversations, dribble a basketball up and down the aisles—these are just a handful of the millions of behaviors people are capable of. All these possible paths vary in how much resistance we run into if we try to follow them. We discover this as soon as we choose paths we're not supposed to. Jump up and start singing, for example, and you'll quickly feel how much resistance other people put up to discourage you from going any further. By comparison, the path of least resistance is far more appealing, which is why it's the one we're most likely to choose.

The odds are loaded toward a path of least resistance in several ways. We often choose a path because it's the only one we see. When I get on an elevator, for example, I turn and face front along with everyone else. It rarely occurs to me to do it any other way, such as facing the rear. If I did, I'd soon feel how some paths bring on more social resistance than others.

I once tested this idea by walking to the rear of an elevator and standing with my back toward the door. As the seconds ticked by, I could feel people looking at me, wondering what I was up to and wanting me to turn around. I wasn't saying anything or doing anything to anyone. I was only standing there minding my own business. But that wasn't all that I was doing, for I was also violating a social norm that makes facing the door a path of least resistance. The path is there all the time—it's built in to riding the elevator as a social situation—but the path wasn't clear until I stepped onto a different one and felt the greater resistance rise up against it.

Similar dynamics operate around issues of privilege. In many corporations, for example, the only way to get promoted is to have a mentor or sponsor pick you out as a promising person and bring you along by teaching you what you need to know and acting as an advocate who opens doors and creates opportunities. In a society that separates and privileges people in various ways, there aren't many opportunities to get comfortable with people across lines of difference. This means that senior managers will feel drawn to employees who resemble them, which usually means those who are white, straight, male, and nondisabled.

Managers who fit this profile probably won't realize they're following a path of least resistance that shapes their choice until they're asked to mentor an African American woman or someone else they don't resemble. The greater resistance toward the path of mentoring across difference may result from something as subtle as feeling "uncomfortable" in the other person's presence. But that's all it takes to make the relationship ineffective or to ensure that it never happens in the first place.[3] And as each manager follows the path to mentor and support those who most resemble them, patterns of privilege and oppression in the system as a whole are perpetuated, regardless of what people consciously feel or intend.

In other cases, people know alternative paths exist, but they stick to the path of least resistance anyway, because they're afraid of what will happen if they don't. Resistance can take many forms, ranging from mild disapproval to being fired from a job, beaten up, run out of town, imprisoned, tortured, or killed. When managers are told to lay off large numbers of workers, for example, they may hate the assignment and feel a huge amount of distress. But the path of *least* resistance is to do what they're told, because the alternative may be to lose their own jobs. To make it less unpleasant, they may use euphemisms like "downsizing" and "outplacement" to soften the painful reality of people losing a way to make a living. (Note in this example how the path of least resistance isn't necessarily an easy path to follow.)

In similar ways, a man may feel uncomfortable when he hears a friend tell a sexist joke and feel compelled to object in some way. But the path of least resistance in that situation is to go along and avoid the risk of being ostracized or ridiculed for challenging his friend and making *him* feel uncomfortable. The path of least resistance is to smile or laugh or just remain silent.

The other half of the relationship between individuals and systems (the left arrow in Figure 2) represents that individuals are the ones who make social systems happen. A college, for example, is a social system, but it doesn't actually happen until students and staff and faculty come together and perform their roles in relation to one another. Since people make systems happen, then people can also make systems happen differently, and when systems happen differently, the consequences are different as well. In 1960, for example, four African American students in Greensboro, North Carolina, entered a Woolworth's lunch counter that, like most such stores across the South, had a policy of not serving people of color. The four students sat down on the stools and asked to see menus, deliberately stepping off the path of least resistance in the hope of forever changing this aspect of the social system. In the days that followed, they were threatened and abused both physically and verbally, but they held their ground and were eventually joined by other students until the sit-in occupied the entire restaurant. Soon, similar actions began in Nashville, Tennessee, and other cities across the South. Within six months, lunch counters in twenty-six cities had been successfully desegregated as well as many other public facilities such as swimming pools and libraries and theaters.[4]

Social life, then, works through the relationship between individuals and social systems and cannot be understood by looking at individuals alone. To see what I mean, consider the game of Monopoly. I used to play Monopoly, but I don't anymore because I don't like the way I behave when I do. Like everyone else, as a Monopoly player I try to win by taking everything from the other players—all their money, all their property—which then forces them out of the game. The point of the game is to ruin everyone else and be the only one left in the end. When you win, you feel good, because you're *supposed* to feel good. Except that one day, I realized that I felt good about winning—about taking everything from everyone else—even when I played against my children, who were pretty young at the time. But there didn't seem to be much point to playing without trying to win, because winning is what the game is *about*. Why land on a property and not buy it, or own a property and not improve it, or have other players land on your property and not collect the rent? So I stopped playing.

And it worked, because the fact is that I don't behave in such greedy ways when I'm not playing Monopoly, even though it's still me, Allan, in either case. So what's all this greedy behavior about? Do we behave in greedy ways simply because we *are* greedy? In a sense, the answer is yes in that greed is part of the human repertoire of possible motivations, just like compassion, altruism, and fear. But how, then, do I explain the absence of such behavior when I'm not playing Monopoly? Clearly, the answer has to include both me as an individual human being who's capable of making all kinds of choices *and* something about the social situation in which I make those choices. It's not one or the other; it's both in relation to each other.

If we think of Monopoly as a social system—as "something larger than ourselves that we participate in"—then we can see how people and systems come together in a dynamic relationship that produces the patterns of social life, including problems surrounding privilege and oppression. People are indisputably the ones who make social systems happen. If no one plays Monopoly, it's just a box full of stuff with writing inside the cover. When people open it up and identify themselves as players, however, Monopoly starts to *happen*. This makes people very important, but we shouldn't confuse that with Monopoly itself. We aren't Monopoly and Monopoly isn't us.

People make Monopoly happen, but *how?* How do we know what to do? How do we choose from the millions of things that, as human beings, we *could* do at any given moment? The answer is the other half of the dynamic relation between individuals and systems. As we sit around the table, we make Monopoly happen from one minute to the next. But our participation in the game also shapes how *we* happen as people—what we think and feel and do. This doesn't mean that systems control us in a rigid and predictable way, as if we were robots or puppets on a string. Instead, systems load the odds in certain directions by laying down paths of least resistance.

Note that the individualistic model cannot explain what's going on, because it would argue that people behave in greedy ways simply because people *are* greedy. But this can't account for the fact that I don't behave in such greedy ways *when I'm not playing Monopoly*. To understand such patterns of behavior, it's not enough to focus just on people's thoughts and feelings, intentions and personalities, because people can and do behave very differently from one social situation to another. When I'm not playing Monopoly, I don't behave in greedy ways, but when I am playing Monopoly, I try to win as much as the next person. Same Allan in each case, but very different behavior and with very different consequences.

What we experience as social life happens through a complex dynamic between systems—families, schools, workplaces, communities, entire societies—and the choices people make as they participate in them and help make them happen. How we experience the world and ourselves, our sense of other people, and the ongoing reality of the systems themselves all arise, take shape, and happen through this dynamic. In this way, social life produces a variety of consequences, including privilege and oppression. To understand that and what we can do to change it, we have to see how systems are organized in ways that encourage people to follow paths of least resistance. The existence of those paths and whether we choose to follow them are keys to what creates and perpetuates all the forms that privilege and oppression can take.

WHAT IT MEANS TO BE INVOLVED IN PRIVILEGE AND OPPRESSION

Individuals and systems are connected to each other through a dynamic relationship. If we use this relationship as a model for thinking about the world and ourselves, it's easier to bring problems such as sexism and ableism out into the open and talk about them. In particular, it's easier to see the problems in relation to us, and to see ourselves in relation to them.

If we think the world is made up of just individuals, then a white woman who's told she's "involved" in racism is going to think you're telling her she's a racist person who harbors ill will toward people of color. She's using an individualistic model of the world that limits her to interpreting words like *racist* as personality flaws. Individualism divides the world up into different kinds of people—good people and bad, racists and nonracists, "good guys" and sexist pigs. It encourages us to think of the isms as diseases that infect people and make them sick. And so we look for a "cure" that will turn diseased, flawed individuals into healthy, "good" ones, or at least isolate them so that they can't infect others. And if we can't cure them, then we can at least try to control their behavior.

But what about everyone else? How do we see *them* in relation to privilege and oppression? What about the vast majority of whites, for example, who tell survey interviewers that they aren't racist and have nothing against people of color? Or what about the majority of men who say they favor an Equal Rights Amendment to the U.S. Constitution? From an individualistic perspective, if you aren't consciously or openly prejudiced or hurtful, then you aren't part of the problem. You might show disapproval of "bad" people and even try to help out the people who are hurt by them. Beyond that, however, the trouble doesn't have anything to do with you so far as you can see. If your feelings and thoughts and outward behavior are good, then *you* are good, and that's all that matters.

Unfortunately, that isn't all that matters. There's more, because patterns of oppression and privilege are rooted in systems that we all participate in and make happen. Those patterns are built into paths of least resistance that people feel drawn to follow every day, regardless of whether they think about where they lead or the consequences they produce. When male professors take more seriously students who look like themselves, for example, they don't have to be self-consciously sexist in order to help perpetuate patterns of male privilege. They don't have to be bad people in order to play a "game" that produces oppressive consequences. It's the same as when people play Monopoly—it always ends with someone winning and everyone else losing, *because that's how the game is set up to work as a system.* The only way to change the outcome is to change how we see and play the game and, eventually, the *system itself* and its paths of least resistance. If we have a vision of what we want social life to look like, we have to create paths that lead in that direction.

Of course there are people in the world who have hatred in their hearts—such as neo-Nazi skinheads who make a sport of harassing and killing people of color or gays or lesbians—and it's important not to minimize the damage they do. Paradoxically, however, even though they cause a lot of trouble, they aren't the key to understanding privilege or doing something about it. They are participating in something larger than themselves that, among other things, steers them toward certain targets for their rage. It's no accident that their hatred is rarely directed at privileged groups but instead at those who are culturally devalued and excluded. Hate-crime perpetrators may have personality disorders that bend them toward victimizing *someone,* but their choice of whom to victimize isn't part of a mental illness. That's something they have to learn, and culture is everyone's most powerful teacher. In choosing targets, they follow paths of least resistance built into a society that everyone participates in, that everyone makes happen, regardless of how they feel or what they intend.

So, if I notice that someone plays Monopoly in a ruthless way, it's a mistake to explain that simply in terms of his or her personality. I also have to ask how a system like Monopoly rewards ruthless behavior more than other games we might play. I have to ask how it creates conditions that make such behavior appear to be the path of least resistance, normal and unremarkable. And since I'm playing the game, too, I'm one of the people who make it happen as a system, and its paths must affect me, too.

My first reaction might be to deny that I follow that path. I'm not a ruthless person or anything close to it. But this misses the key difference between systems and the people who participate in them: We don't have to be ruthless *people* in order to support or follow paths of least resistance that lead to behavior with ruthless *consequences.* After all, we're all trying to win, because that's the point of the game. However gentle and kind I am as I take your money when you land on my Boardwalk with its four houses, take it I will and gladly, too. "Thank you," I say in my most sincerely unruthless tone, or even "Sorry," as I drive you out of the game by taking your last dollar and your mortgaged properties. Me, ruthless? Not at all. I'm just playing the game the way it's supposed to be played. And even if I don't try hard to win, the mere fact that I play the game supports its existence and makes it possible, especially if I remain silent about the consequences it produces. Just my going along makes the game appear normal and acceptable, which reinforces the paths of least resistance for everyone else.

This is how most systems work and how most people participate in them. It's also how systems of privilege work. Good people with good intentions make systems happen in ways that produce all kinds of injustice and suffering for people in culturally devalued and excluded groups. Most of the time, people don't even know the paths are there in the first place, and this is why it's important to raise awareness that everyone is always following them in one way or another. If you weren't following a path of least resistance, you'd certainly know it, because you'd be on an alternative path with greater resistance that would make itself felt. In other words, if you're not going along with the system, it won't be long before people notice and let you know it. All you have to do is show up someplace wearing "inappropriate" clothes to see how quickly resistance can form around alternative paths.

The trouble around privilege and oppression is so pervasive, so long-standing, so huge in its consequences for so many millions of people that it can't be written off as the misguided doings of a small percentage of people with personality problems. The people who get labeled as racists or homophobes, for example, are all following racist, heterosexist paths of least resistance that are built into the entire society.

In a way, "bad people" are like ruthless Monopoly players who are doing just what the game calls for even if their "style" is a bit extreme. Such extremists may be the ones who grab the headlines, but they don't have enough power to create and sustain trouble of this magnitude. The trouble appears in the daily routines of every workplace, every school and university, every government agency, every community. It involves every major kind of social system, and since systems don't exist without the involvement of people, there's no way to escape being involved in the trouble that comes out of them. If we participate in systems the trouble comes out of, and if those systems exist only through our participation, then this is enough to involve us in the trouble itself.

Reminders of this reality are everywhere. I see it, for example, every time I look at the label in a piece of clothing. I just went upstairs to my closet and noted where each of my shirts was made. Although each carries a U.S. brand name, only three were made here. The rest were made in the Philippines, Thailand, Mexico, Taiwan, Macao, Singapore, or Hong Kong. And although each cost me twenty to forty dollars, it's a good bet that the people who actually made them—

primarily women—were paid pennies for their labor performed under terrible conditions that can resemble slavery.

The only reason people exploit workers in such horrible ways is to make money in a capitalist system. To judge from the contents of my closet, that clearly includes some of *my* money. By itself, that fact doesn't make me a bad person, because I certainly don't intend people to suffer for the sake of my wardrobe. But it does mean I'm involved in their suffering because I participate in a system that produces it. As someone who helps make the system happen, however, I can also be a part of the solution.

But isn't the difference I could make a tiny one? The question makes me think of the devastating floods of 1993 along the Mississippi and Missouri rivers. The news was full of powerful images of people from all walks of life working feverishly side by side to build dikes to hold back the raging waters that threatened their communities. Together, they filled and placed thousands of sandbags. When the waters receded, much had been lost, but a great deal had been saved as well. I wonder how it felt to be one of those people. I imagine they were proud of their effort and experienced a satisfying sense of solidarity with the people they'd worked with. The sandbags each individual personally contributed were the tiniest fraction of the total, but each felt part of the group effort and was proud to identify with the consequences it produced. They didn't have to make a big or even measurable difference to feel involved.

It works that way with the good things that come out of people pulling together in all the systems that make up social life. It also works that way with the bad things, with each sandbag adding to the problem instead of the solution. To perpetuate privilege and oppression, we don't even have to do anything consciously to support it. Just our silence is crucial for ensuring its future, for the simple fact is that no system of privilege can continue to exist without most people choosing to remain silent about it. If most heterosexuals spoke out about heterosexism, for example, or if most nondisabled people came out of their closet of silence and stood openly against ableism, it would be a critical first step toward revolutionary change. But the vast majority of "good" people are silent on these issues, and it's easy for others to read their silence as support.

As long as we participate in social systems, we don't get to choose whether to be involved in the consequences they produce. We're involved simply through the fact that we're here. As such, we can only choose *how* to be involved, whether to be just part of the problem or also to be part of the solution. That's where our power lies, and also our responsibility.

CHAPTER 7

How Systems of Privilege Work

Like everything else in social life, privilege and oppression exist only through social systems and people's participation in them. People make systems and their consequences happen through paths of least resistance that shape who people are and how they participate. To see how all that works, we need to look at how systems are put together. If we look at the game of Monopoly as a system, for example, we can describe it without ever talking about the personalities of the people who might play it. We can do the same thing with a university, a corporation, a family, a society, or a world economic system like global capitalism.

Systems organized around privilege have three key characteristics. They are *dominated* by privileged groups, *identified* with privileged groups, and *centered* on privileged groups. All three characteristics support the idea that members of privileged groups are superior to those below them and, therefore, deserve their privilege. A patriarchy, for example, is male-dominated, male-identified, and male-centered.[1] Race privilege happens through systems that are white-dominated, white-identified, and white-centered, and ableism works through systems that are dominated, identified with, and centered on nondisabled people.

DOMINANCE

When we say that a system is dominated by a privileged group, it means that positions of power tend to be occupied by members of that group. Power also tends to be identified with such people in ways that make it seem normal and natural for them to have it.

In a patriarchy, for example, power is culturally gendered in that it is associated primarily with men. To the people living in such a society, power looks "natural" on a man but unusual and even problematic on a woman, marking her as an exception that calls for special scrutiny and some kind of explanation. When Margaret Thatcher was prime minister of Great Britain, for example, she was often referred to as "the Iron Lady." This drew attention to both her strength as a leader and the need to mark it as an exception. There would be no such need to mark a strong male prime minister (as an "Iron Man," for example), because his power would be assumed.

This kind of thinking supports a structure that allocates most power to men. In almost every organization, the farther down you look in the power structure, the more numerous women are. The higher up you go, the fewer women you'll find. That's what a male-dominated system looks like.

Just because a system is male-dominated doesn't mean all men are powerful. As most men will tell you, they aren't, most often because of class or race or disability status. Male dominance does mean, however, that every man can *identify* with power as a value that his culture associates with manhood, and this identification makes it easier for any man to assume and use power in relation to others. It also encourages a sense of entitlement in men to use women to meet their personal needs, whether it's getting coffee for everyone or taking the minutes of a meeting. Since women are culturally *dis*identified with power, it's harder for them to exercise it in any situation. When women do find ways to be powerful in relation to men, it's usually *in spite of* the male-dominated character of patriarchal systems as a whole.

For women to have power in relation to men also makes women vulnerable, because power in their hands lacks the cultural legitimacy of men's power. As such, it easily arouses suspicion. Female professors, for example, often tell stories of having their authority, expertise, and professional commitment routinely challenged not only by colleagues but also by students, men in particular.[2] As a man, I enjoy the benefit of the doubt with students, who usually assume I know what I'm talking about. When a woman walks into the same classroom, however, male students may challenge her credibility and authority from the start, arguing or questioning every point and feeling free to interrupt her. They may go so far as to comment on her physical appearance or turn away, roll their eyes, go to sleep, hold side conversations.

"I'm still routinely asked if I've ever taught the course before," says one seasoned female professor. "They look utterly shocked when I say I've taught most of my courses 15–18 years—sometimes longer than they've been alive."[3]

Similar things can happen with peers. After teaching her first class, a new professor saw a male faculty member poke his head into her classroom after the students left. "Are you a faculty member here?" he asked.

"Yes," she said.

"Do you have a doctorate?"

"Yes."

"Well, at least you're educated," he said, and walked away.[4]

Powerful women are also open to being called bitches or lesbians as a way to discredit and negate their power by attacking them personally. When women gather together, even just for lunch, men may suspect them of "being up to something"—planning some subversive use of power that needs to be monitored and contained. Men's anxiety over this usually comes out as humor ("So, what little plot are you hatching?"), but the gender dynamic underlying male dominance and women's potential to subvert it is clearly there. In the home—the one place where women manage to carve out some power for themselves—their power is routinely seen as problematic in ways that men's power in relation to women is not. The abundance of insulting terms for men who are dominated by women, for example, and the absence of such insults for comparable women show clearly how our culture legitimizes male dominance.

That patriarchy is male-dominated also doesn't mean that most men have domineering personalities and need or want to control others. In other words, I'm not using the term *male dominance* to describe men.

Rather, it describes a patriarchal system in which both men and women participate. It also describes gendered patterns of unequal power and paths of least resistance for both men and women that support those patterns.

For men, paths of least resistance include presenting the appearance of being in control of themselves, others, and events. I'm aware of this path, for example, in how I feel drawn to respond to questions whether I know the answer or not, to interrupt in conversations, to avoid admitting that I'm wrong about anything, to take up room in public spaces. One day some years ago, my life partner Nora Jamieson and I were having a conversation about something that began when she raised a question. I responded almost without hesitation, until she interrupted me to ask, "Do you actually know that or are you just saying it?" I was startled to realize that I was just saying it. The response appeared in my head and that seemed reason enough to say it. But I wasn't saying it as though it was just a thought that happened to be wandering through my mind. I spoke with an unhesitating flow that suggested I knew what I was talking about, that I was an expert in the subject she'd raised.

But I didn't know that what I was saying was true, at least no more true than what anyone else might say, provided, of course, that I gave them the chance. This included Nora, who had been sitting there listening to me in silence. Until that moment, she followed a corresponding path of least resistance for women: silent attentiveness, hesitation, self-doubt, humility, deference, supporting what men say and do, and taking up as little space as possible. When she stepped off that path, she shook an entire structure by revealing its existence and how both of us were participating in it. She also raised the possibility of alternative paths—of men learning about silence and listening, doubt and uncertainty, supporting others and sharing space.

Why call such patterns of control and deference "paths of least resistance"? Why not just say that I and many other men have a problem we might call a "controlling personality" or that women just tend to be "unassertive"? The answer is that we all swim in a dominant culture that is full of images of men seeking control, taking up time and space, competing with other men, and living with a sense of entitlement in relation to women. And each of those is matched by images of women letting men do all of that, if not encouraging them to or insisting on it. The images permeate popular culture—from film and television to advertising and literature—and shape the news, from the front page to the sports section.

What these images do is place a value on male power and control that is used every day as a standard for evaluating men in almost every aspect of their lives. Men who live up to it are routinely rewarded with approval, while men who seem insufficiently decisive and manly are always vulnerable to ridicule and scorn, primarily from other men. And so if I feel drawn to control a conversation or to always have an answer, it isn't simply because I'm a controlling *person,* no more than greedy behavior happens in a Monopoly game just because people are greedy.

This is what Deborah Tannen misses in her popular books on gender and talk.[5] She describes many gender differences in styles of talking that tend to give men control over conversations. But when she tries to explain why this is so, she almost completely ignores how those differences promote male privilege at women's expense. Instead, she argues that women and men talk differently because as children they played in same-sex groups and learned distinctively male or female ways of speaking from their peers. What she doesn't tell us is how those peers happened to acquire their gendered styles of talking. The answer is that they learned them from adults in families, the mass media, and in school. In other words, they learned them by participating in a society where conversation is a major arena in which male privilege is played out.

Patterns of dominance and the paths of least resistance that sustain them show up in every system of privilege. White dominance, for example, is reflected in an unequal racial balance of power in society and its institutions. The same is true of heterosexuality, although so many lesbians and gay men are still in the closet that it's hard to be sure about the sexual orientation of people in power. There is no ambiguity or lack of clarity in the mainstream culture, however. It's rare to see a film or a television show in which the most powerful character is identified as gay, lesbian, with a disability, working class, or African American, Latino/a, or Asian, or if they are, to have them still be alive when the closing credits begin to roll. Working-class characters are rarely the focus in films and on television, and when they do appear they are routinely portrayed as criminals or as stupid, ignorant, crude, bigoted, shallow, and immoral.[6] The closest that people of color get to powerful roles is as sidekicks to powerful whites in "buddy" movies. Exceptions like *The Color Purple* and *The Manchurian Candidate* are few and far between. And in a heterosexist culture, a powerful gay man is a contradiction in terms, and powerful lesbians are often dismissed as not being real women at all.

The result of such patterns of dominance is that if you're female, of color, or in some other way on the outside of privilege, when you look upward in all kinds of power structures you don't see people like you. Your interests are not represented where power is wielded and rewards are distributed, and you get no encouragement to imagine yourself as one of those with access to power and its rewards. Those who don't look like people in power will feel invisible and in fact *be* invisible, because they are routinely overlooked. And this is a major way that patterns of inequality and privilege repeat themselves over and over again.

IDENTIFIED WITH PRIVILEGE

"It's a man's world" is an expression that points in part to the male-dominated character of society that puts most power in the hands of men. In the same way, one could say, "It's a white world" or "a straight world" or a "nondisabled world." But there's more than power at work here, because privileged groups are also usually taken as the standard of comparison that represents the best that society has to offer. This is what it means to say that a system is male-identified or white-identified.

On most college campuses, for example, students of color feel pressured to talk, dress, and act like middle-class whites in order to fit in and be accepted.[7] In similar ways, most workplaces define appropriate appearance and ways of speaking in terms that are culturally associated with being white, from clothing and hairstyles to diction and slang. People of color often experience being marked as outsiders, to the extent that many navigate the social world by consciously changing how they talk from one situation to another. In shopping for an apartment over the telephone, for example, many African Americans know they have to "talk white" in order to be accepted (which may come to nothing once they show up in person and discover that the apartment has "just" been rented).[8]

Because privileged groups are assumed to represent society as a whole, "American" is culturally defined as white, in spite of the diversity of the population. You can see this in a statement like "Americans must learn to be more tolerant of other races." I doubt that most people would see this as saying that we need Asians to be more tolerant of whites or blacks to be more tolerant of Native Americans. The "Americans" are assumed to be white, and the "other races" are assumed to be races *other* than white. *Other* is the key word in understanding how systems are identified with privileged groups. The privileged group is the assumed "we" in relation to "them." The "other" is the "you people" whom the "we" regard as problematic, unacceptable, unlikable, or beneath "our" standards.

Note, by the way, how such assumptions operate on a larger scale in my use of the word "American" in the preceding paragraph. People in the United States routinely refer to themselves as Americans, as if "America" and "United States" mean the same thing. But they do not: "America" refers to the entire western hemisphere—South America, Central America, and North America—and "American" includes a wide variety of societies in addition to our own. The assumption in U.S. culture that only citizens of the United States are Americans encourages the perception of everyone else as some kind of "other" and reflects dynamics of privilege and oppression in relations among nations.

In a white-identified system, white is the assumed race unless something other than white is marked—hence the common use of the term *nonwhite* to lump together various peoples of color into a single category of "other" in relation to a white standard. To get a sense of the effect of this practice, imagine a society in which whites were referred to routinely as "noncoloreds."

White identification means that whether arrested for a crime or winning a Nobel prize, whites are rarely if ever identified *as* white, because that is assumed. Racial tags are common, however, for everyone else, from "black physician" and "Latina writer" to "Asian actor."

If a small group of white citizens marched on Washington to protest a policy that had nothing to do with race, news reports wouldn't mention their race and certainly wouldn't try to figure out why the group was all white. They would simply be described as protesters or citizens or members of a group that takes a position on that policy. If a group of Chicanas/os did the same thing, they would surely be identified as such and be asked why there weren't any whites among them. And this isn't because Chicanas/os stand out as a numerical minority, since the same pattern would hold for women, who would "stand out" and be tagged as women even though they outnumber men in the population.

Such patterns of identification are especially powerful in relation to gender. It is still common to use masculine pronouns to refer to people in general or to use *man* to refer both to males and to the entire species (as in "mankind" and "the family of man"). In a similar way, men and manhood are held up as standards of comparison. The idea of "brotherhood," for example, is clearly gendered, since women can't be brothers by any stretch of the imagination, yet it also carries powerful cultural meaning about *human* connection, as in the stirring line from *America the Beautiful,* "And crown thy good with brotherhood from sea to shining sea."[9] Brotherhood is defined as a "condition" or a "quality" of human relationship (see Box 1) that embodies warmth and good feeling, especially across social differences. It is linked to the idea of *fellowship*—the general human capacity for companionship, common interest or feeling, friendliness, and communion—which is based on being a fellow, which is also clearly and unambiguously defined as male. By comparison, although African American women have made powerful use of the idea of sisterhood, in the dominant patriarchal culture it amounts to little more than the biological fact of being someone's sister, which is to say, being female and sharing the same set of parents. All its other meanings are narrowly confined to groups of women—such as nuns and feminists—even when it refers to the quality of relationships.

In short, men are the cultural standard for humanity, and women are just women. So, when a woman is celebrated at the office and everyone joins in a round of "For She's a Jolly Good Fellow," no one laughs or objects to the oxymoron, because in a male-identified society, it's

---

Box 1
The Word "Brotherhood" as
an Instance of Male-Identified Language

Sisterhood	Brotherhood
1. The state of being a sister.	1. The condition or quality of being a brother.
2. A group of sisters, especially of nuns or of female members of a church.	2. The quality of being brotherly, **fellow**ship.
3. An organization of women with a common interest.	3. A fraternal or trade organization.
4. Congenial relationship or companionship among women.	4. All those engaged in a particular trade or profession or sharing a common interest or quality.
5. Community or network of women who participate in support of feminism.	5. The belief that all people should act with warmth and equality toward one another regardless of differences in race, creed, nationality, etc.

Fellow	Fellowship
A man or boy.	1. The condition or relation of being a fellow; the fellowship of humankind.
	2. Friendly relationship.

---

an honor to be considered "one of the guys," to be associated with men and the standards by which men are measured. Nor are many people disturbed by the fact that there are *no* words that culturally associate women with a valued quality of human relation in the way that *fellow* and *fellowship* do for men. If someone suggested changing the words of *America the Beautiful* to "and crown thy good with sisterhood," however, imagine the reception that idea would get and you have some idea of the power of male identification.

Male identification is woven into every aspect of social life. Most high-status occupations, for example, are organized around qualities culturally associated with masculinity, such as aggression, competitiveness, emotional detachment (except for anger), and control. This is what it takes to succeed in law, medicine, science, academia, politics, sports, or business. No woman (or man) becomes a corporate manager, gets tenure at a university, or is elected to public office by showing their capacity for cooperation, sharing, emotional sensitivity, and nurturing. This also applies to the most highly rewarded blue-collar jobs, such as police work, firefighting, and skilled construction trades.

This means that a man can make it as a lawyer or a manager while at the same time living up to the cultural standards that define a "real man." A woman, however, is in a bind. If she patterns herself on ideals that are culturally defined as feminine, she's likely to be seen as not having what it takes to get ahead in a male-identified world. But if she pursues a more "masculine" path toward success, she opens herself to being judged as not feminine enough—uncaring, cold, a bitch. Students usually hold their female college professors, for example, to a higher standard of caring and emotional availability than they do male teachers. But if a woman professional comes across as *too* warm and caring, her credibility, competence, and authority are invariably undermined and challenged. In a male-identified system, she can't fit the model of a successful professional or manager and at the same time measure up as a "real woman." It is the kind of classic double bind that is one of the hallmarks of social oppression—she can be devalued no matter what she does.[10]

The world of work is also male-identified in the definition of a "career" and the timing of key stages in the route to success. In most organizations, for example, the idea of a career assumes an almost complete commitment to the work, which means that the only way to have both a career and a family is to have someone at home to take care of children and other domestic responsibilities. Despite all the talk about "the new fatherhood," this almost always means a wife and mother. Furthermore, in typical patterns of career timing, the key years for establishing yourself overlap with a woman's key years for starting a family. In this way, "serious" work is structured to fit most men's lives far more easily and with far less conflict than it fits most women's lives.[11] So *profession* and *career* are words that on the surface don't appear to be gendered one way or the other but are in fact implicitly male-identified.

Male identification shows up in more subtle ways as well, from popular culture to the comings and goings of everyday life. In Ken Burns's PBS documentary on baseball, for example, he tells us: "Baseball defines who we are." Apparently, he didn't give much thought to who is included in *we*. I doubt he meant that the essence of baseball defines who women are in some fundamental way or that it defines what most women experience as their society. But if the statement is likely to ring true for men, then, in a male-identified world, it's assumed that it rings true for everyone, and if it doesn't, so what?

In this way, male identification tends to make women invisible, just as white and nondisabled identification tends to make people of color and people with disabilities invisible. The other day I made an airline reservation and the clerk gave me a confirmation code. "PWCEO," she said, and then, to make sure I'd gotten it right, added, "That's Peter, William, Charles, Edward, Oscar."

PRIVILEGE AT THE CENTER

Because systems are identified with privileged groups, the path of least resistance is to focus attention on them—who they are, what they do and say, and how they do it. Look at the front page of any newspaper, and you'll find that the vast majority of people pictured, quoted, and discussed are men who also happen to be white and middle or upper class. If white women, Latinos/as, or African Americans are there, it's usually because of something that's been done to them (murdered, for example) or something they've done wrong (rioted, murdered, stole, cheated, and so on). There are exceptions, of course—a Condoleezza Rice as National Security Advisor or a Colin Powell as Secretary of State or black athletes—one of the few areas where they are allowed to excel. As exceptions, however, they prove the rule.

To judge from television and film, most of what happens of significance in the world happens to straight white nondisabled men. To see what I mean, try an experiment: Make a list of the ten most important movies ever made, movies that reflect something powerful and enduring about the human experience, about courage and personal transformation, the journey of the soul, the testing of character, finding

---

Box 2
Academy Award Winning Films in the
Category "Best Picture," 1965–2003

2003 *Lord of the Rings*	1983 *Terms of Endearment*
2002 *Chicago*	1982 *Gandhi*
2001 *A Beautiful Mind*	1981 *Chariots of Fire*
2000 *Gladiator*	1980 *Ordinary People*
1999 *American Beauty*	1979 *Kramer vs. Kramer*
1998 *Shakespeare in Love*	1978 *The Deer Hunter*
1997 *Titanic*	1977 *Annie Hall*
1996 *The English Patient*	1976 *Rocky*
1995 *Braveheart*	1975 *One Flew Over the*
1994 *Forrest Gump*	*Cuckoo's Nest*
1993 *Schindler's List*	1974 *The Godfather, Part II*
1992 *Unforgiven*	1973 *The Sting*
1991 *The Silence of the Lambs*	1972 *The Godfather, Part I*
1990 *Dances with Wolves*	1971 *The French Connection*
1989 *Driving Miss Daisy*	1970 *Patton*
1988 *Rain Man*	1969 *Midnight Cowboy*
1987 *The Last Emperor*	1968 *Oliver!*
1986 *Platoon*	1967 *In the Heat of the Night*
1985 *Out of Africa*	1966 *A Man for All Seasons*
1984 *Amadeus*	1965 *The Sound of Music*

---

out who we really are and what life is all about. Once you have your list, identify the key character in each, the one whose courage, transformation, journey, testing, and revelations are the point of the story. Chances are that at least nine out of ten will be white, Anglo, nondisabled heterosexual males, even though they constitute less than 20 percent of the U.S. population.

Consider, for example, the list of films that have been awarded the Oscar for best picture over the last forty years (see Box 2). Of these films, judged better than all the rest in each year, none set in the United States places people of color at the center of the story without their having to share it with white characters of equal importance (*Driving Miss Daisy* and *In the Heat of the Night*). The one film that focuses on Native Americans (*Dances with Wolves*) is told from a white man's point of view with Native Americans clearly identified as the other. Only two focus on non-European cultures (*The Last Emperor* and *Gandhi*). Although *Out of Africa* is set in Africa, the story focuses exclusively on whites and, without any critical comment, their exploitation of the African continent. This same list of films also contains only four that are female-centered (*Chicago, Out of Africa, Terms of Endearment,* and *The Sound of Music*) and none with any major characters who are gay or lesbian.

When a film does focus on someone in a subordinate group, it gets little attention unless, like *The Color Purple* (1985), it has a powerful white heterosexual male such as Steven Spielberg behind it. Anything less than that—no matter how good it is—has little chance of drawing much attention, much less winning an Academy Award. Even *The Color Purple,* which was nominated for eleven Academy Awards, didn't win a single one, losing to *Out of Africa.*

The handful of films that do focus on people in subordinate groups are likely to be tagged (and devalued) as "women's films" ("chick flicks") or "black films" or "gay films" or "lesbian films," even though all the rest are never called "men's films" or "white films" or "heterosexual films." In a society identified with dominant groups, such films are supposedly about everyone, or at least everyone who counts.

Films that focus on people with disabilities—*Rain Man, Forrest Gump,* and *A Beautiful Mind*—reflect an important aspect of this phenomenon. While the main character in each film has a disability, in every case the story is *about* the disability, rather than being a human story that happens to be told through the life of a character who has a disability. Similar things happen with films that focus on people of color—*In the Heat of the Night* and *Driving Miss Daisy* both have race as a central focus of the story. And if there is ever an Academy Award winning film whose main character is gay or lesbian, we can be sure that sexual orientation will be its major theme. Not so, however, with films that focus on members of dominant groups.

Because systems of privilege center on dominant groups, those who aren't included have reason to feel invisible, because in an important social sense, they are. Black, Latino/a, and white female students routinely report that instructors don't call on them in class, don't listen to what they say, or don't let them finish without interruption.

Research shows that men receive the overwhelming majority of attention in classrooms at every level of education,[12] a pattern that repeats itself in the workplace and everywhere else that women and men meet. I've been in meetings of thirty people in which the two or three men present talked almost the entire time with no sign from anyone that anything was wrong.

This happens in part because in a world that centers attention on men and what they do and say, the path of least resistance for men is to claim attention by calling out answers without being recognized, for example, or by interrupting women. It also happens because the path of least resistance for women is to give way in the face of male privilege, to allow men to take up whatever time and space they want and not challenge their right to do so. So, when male students jump in with a response—even to the extent of thinking up answers as they go along—teachers and female students will often let them get away with it.

When men don't jump in, teachers tend to gravitate toward them anyway, standing closer to them in the room, looking to them for the most interesting or productive answers, challenging and coaching them more, all the while assuming women don't have what it takes to say something worth hearing.[13] None of this has to be done consciously in order to center attention on dominant groups at the expense of everyone else. It simply flows along down a well-traveled path of least resistance that makes invisibility a key part of the devaluing that lies at the heart of privilege and oppression.

Often the only way marginalized groups can get attention is to make an issue of how social life is centered on dominant groups. So women form their own support groups at work or attend women's colleges where they don't have to overcome the cultural weight of male-centeredness. Blacks form their own dorms or clubs on college campuses and sit at their own tables in the dining hall.[14] Schools create special programs that focus on women or peoples of color. Women participate in a "Take Our Daughters to Work" day, or lesbians and gay men organize pride marches to draw attention to the simple fact that they exist ("We are everywhere").

Drawing attention away from dominant groups often provokes a defensive response that reaffirms privilege. In systems of privilege, the focus is on dominant groups all the time as a matter of course, so much that it's never recognized as something special. The slightest deviation, then, can be perceived as a loss of privilege. Some fascinating research, for example, shows that as long as men overwhelmingly dominate the conversation, the participation of women and men is perceived as *roughly equal*. But if women's talk rises to as little as a quarter or a third of the total interaction, men tend to perceive the women as taking over. Such perceived shifts can result in howls of protest over the unfairness of giving subordinate groups "special" attention—"Why not a 'Take Our Sons to Work Day'?" "Why do gays and lesbians have to call attention to themselves?" "When do we get to have a White History Month?"

As so often happens, subordinate groups are in a double bind. If they don't call attention to themselves, the defaults built into systems of privilege make them invisible and devalued. If they do call attention to themselves, if they dare to put themselves at the center, they risk being accused of being pushy or seeking special treatment. This is why women and people of color, for example, are often labeled as "special-interest groups" with biased agendas, whereas men and whites are not.

THE ISMS

Most of the time, words like *racism, sexism, ableism,* and *heterosexism* are used to describe how people feel and behave. Racism, for example, is seen as something that exists only inside people as a flawed part of their personalities. It's an attitude, a collection of stereotypes, a bad intention, a desire or need to discriminate or do harm, a form of hatred. From that perspective, doing something about racism means changing how individuals feel, think, and behave (since behavior is connected to how we think and feel).

But racism is also built in to the systems that people live and work in. It's embedded in a capitalist system organized around competition over scarce resources, and organized to be white-dominated, white-identified, and white-centered. This manifests itself everywhere we turn. Given this reality, it doesn't make sense to ignore everything but individual personality and behavior, as if we live in a social vacuum. For this reason, sociologist David Wellman argues for a broader definition of racism that includes but goes beyond the personal. Racism is the patterns of privilege and oppression themselves and *anything*—intentional or not—that helps to create or perpetuate those patterns. If we extend this to other forms of privilege, then sexism and ableism and heterosexism are also more than personal expressions of hostility or prejudice but include everything that people do or don't do that promotes those forms of privilege.[15]

To see what Wellman means, consider not what people do or say, but what they don't. Consider, for example, the power of silence to promote privilege and oppression. Human beings are highly dependent on one another for standards of what—and who—is okay and who isn't. Although there will always be individuals who don't care what other people think, the vast majority will avoid doing something they believe people around them would criticize. But if people in their community and society are silent, then the perpetrators are free to interpret that as support for what they do.

From the late 1800s through the mid-1940s, for example, white Southerners lynched more than three thousand African Americans.[16] The actual violence was done by a relatively small number of individuals, but they acted from the assumption that most people in their communities and states either approved of their actions or wouldn't do anything to stop them even if they disapproved. Many lynchings were advertised in advance in local newspapers, for example, and pictures taken of the atrocities were often sold as postcards.

Since the lynchers couldn't possibly know everyone in their community or state personally, the only way they could assume they'd get away with it was to see themselves as living in a particular kind of society—white-dominated, white-identified, and white-centered—that placed such a low value on black people's lives that torturing and killing them was unlikely to be made an issue, much less treated as a crime. The real power lay not with the lynchers as individuals but with society and the great collective silence in the face of the racist horror the individuals perpetrated, a silence that spoke as loudly as the violence itself, regardless of how people felt about it as individuals.

Just as most Southerners (and Northerners) were silent about lynching, the vast majority of men are silent on the issue of sexual harassment and violence and do nothing more than privately disapprove of it or assure themselves that they'd never engage in it themselves. In the same way, most whites do nothing to raise consciousness about all the ways racism works in their communities or workplaces. They may readily acknowledge overt behavior that perpetuates privilege and oppression. "Yes," they'll say when asked about discrimination, "it's a terrible thing." And they mean it.

What they don't see most of the time, however, is how silence and not looking and not asking are *in effect* just as racist *because oppression depends on this in order to continue.* White professors or managers who don't go out of their way to ask about race in classrooms or the workplace may be good people who'd never act from ill will toward people of color. But how good or bad they are as people is beside the point. Their motives and intentions are irrelevant to the future of racism as a pattern of inequality and the suffering it causes. What counts isn't just what they do, but even more what they *don't* do.[17]

When I think about this, I imagine a scene in which a gang of white men are beating a person of color in broad daylight on a city street. I'm standing in a crowd of white people who are watching. We aren't hurting anyone. We feel no ill will toward the man being beaten and may feel sorry for him. We aren't cheering the attackers on or showing any outward signs of approval. We're just standing in silence, "minding our own business." And then one of the men stops, looks up, and says, his eyes panning across our faces, "We appreciate your support. We couldn't do this without you."

This is how racism and other forms of privilege really work day in and day out. It results from what is called "passive oppression," which can be defined as making it possible for oppression to happen simply by doing nothing to stop it. Privilege and oppression depend on a social environment that makes it easy for so many to stand by and do nothing. Most white people in the United States engage in racism not by acting from feelings or thoughts of racial hostility or ill will but "because they acquiesce in the large cultural order that continues the work of racism."[18] That's all that's required of most white people for racism to continue—that they not notice, that they do nothing, that they remain silent.

THE ISMS AND US

It is tempting for members of dominant groups to suppose they could be raised in a society organized around privilege and participate in it day after day without being touched by it on a personal level. But it's a dream that, for everyone else, is a nightmare of denial. There is no way for a member of a dominant group to escape that kind of immersion unscathed. Nobody is the exception who miraculously doesn't internalize any of the negative ideas, attitudes, or images that pour in a steady stream from the surrounding culture and make privilege and oppression happen as they do.

In other words, on some level, *of course* I've internalized aspects of racism, sexism, ableism, and heterosexism in myself in the same way that I automatically dream in English and prefer certain foods. I wish it weren't so, but it is. The assumption that some racism resides in every white person, for example, is a reasonable one in this society.[19] I would assume that everyone I meet in the United States speaks English until I was showed otherwise, not because of what I know about them, but because of what I know about the culture of this society. In the same way, I would assume that racism touches and shapes everyone in one way or another and leaves a mark that cannot be erased. To assume otherwise is to engage in wishful thinking and live in a world that doesn't exist.

Having privilege doesn't mean someone is a bad person. But it does mean that there isn't a single member of a dominant group who doesn't have issues of privilege to deal with both internally and externally, in relation to the world around them. It was handed to them when they were children with no sense of what was wise and good to take into themselves and what was not. And so they accepted it, uncritically, unknowingly, even innocently, but accept it they did. It wasn't their fault. They have no reason to feel guilty about it, because they didn't *do* anything. But now it is there for them to deal with, just as it's there for women, people of color, people with disabilities, lesbians, and gay men who *also* didn't do anything to deserve the oppression that so profoundly shapes their lives.

CHAPTER 8

Getting Off the Hook: Denial and Resistance

No one likes to see themselves as connected to someone else's misery, no matter how remote the link. Usually their first response
is to find a way to get themselves off the hook, and, as I'll show below,
there are all kinds of ways to do that. As a result, they leave it to someone else to take care of the problem, which, of course, doesn't happen, and for pretty much the same reasons.

The fact is that we're all on the hook because there's no way to
avoid being part of the problem. People in subordinate groups are on
the hook every day. Dominant groups are, too, but they're more likely
not to know it because they have so many ways to act as though they
aren't, and privilege usually allows them to get away with it. But the
more aware we are of all the ways there are to fool ourselves, the easier it is to wake up and make ourselves part of the solution.[1]

DENY AND MINIMIZE

Perhaps the easiest way to get off the hook is to deny that it exists
in the first place.

"Racism and sexism used to be problems, but they aren't anymore."

"The American Dream is alive and well and available to everyone."

"There are no people with disabilities where I work, so that isn't an issue here."

"Affirmative action has actually turned the tables—if anyone's in trouble now, it's whites and men." Or, as a cover of the *Atlantic Monthly* magazine proclaimed, "Girls Rule!"[2]

Closely related to denial is the minimization of the trouble by acknowledging that it exists but then claiming that it doesn't amount to much. When women and people of color are accused of "whining," for example, they're essentially being told that whatever they have to deal with isn't that bad and they should "just get on with it." When you deny the reality of oppression, you also deny the reality of the privilege that underlies it, which is just what it takes to get off the hook.

When people in dominant groups practice this kind of denial, it rarely seems to occur to them that they're in a poor position to know what they're talking about. For them to act as though they know better than others do about what they are up against is just the sort of presumption that privilege encourages. Privilege invites them to define other people's experience for them, to tell them what it's like to be them regardless of what they say it's like. Adults do this all the time with children. A child falls down and cries and an adult might say, "Now, now, stop crying, it doesn't hurt that much," when in fact the adult doesn't know just how much it hurts. Or the child wakes up with a nightmare and adults might tell them, "There's nothing to be afraid of," when that may not be true at all for the child. In similar ways, members of privileged groups are culturally authorized to interpret other people's experience for them, to deny the validity of their own reports, and to impose their views of reality.

Denial also takes the form of seeing subordinate groups as actually being *better off* than privileged groups. I once knew a woman, for example, who often remarked with a sense of envy on the qualities black people have had to develop to survive in the face of centuries of racism. She sees in them a strength and depth of soul and feeling that she'd like to have herself. Whenever the subject of racism comes up, her first response is to counter with a list of black "advantages," as if weighing them in the balance against her privileged position as a white woman. Her tone is a mixture of longing and resentment, as if she feels put upon to have to consider white privilege for even a moment when she feels such a lack in her own life. The paradoxical idea that envy and privilege can and often do exist side by side doesn't occur to her as she defends herself against seeing what she'd rather not see.

As Stanley Cohen argues in his book, *States of Denial,* when it becomes impossible to avoid seeing the reality of privilege and oppression, additional levels of denial come into play—not feeling anything about it or feeling something but not seeing it as a moral issue or, if all else fails, denying there's anything we can do.[3]

BLAME THE VICTIM

One can acknowledge that terrible things happen to people and still get off the hook by blaming it all on them.[4] Whites can draw on a rich supply of negative cultural stereotypes, for example, to satisfy themselves that if people of color were different—if they were more like whites supposedly are—they wouldn't have so much trouble. Whites can say things such as "If blacks were smarter or worked harder or got an education, they'd be okay" and expect most other whites to go along, because racist stereotypes have such authority in this culture. They can also count on whites who disagree with them not to say so to their face.

In similar ways, men can tell themselves that women who say they're sexually harassed are hypersensitive, or had no business being where they were, or sent mixed signals, or "asked for it" in one way or another. If a woman fails to break through the glass ceiling, men can say she doesn't have the right stuff. If she allows herself to be openly emotional, men can point to that as a reason she hasn't reached the heights. If she *isn't* emotional and nurturing, they can criticize her for not being "womanly" enough, too much like a man. If she's friendly, men can say she wants to be approached sexually. If she isn't friendly, they can say she's stuck up, cold, a bitch even, and deserves whatever she gets.

Or people with disabilities are told that the reason they can't get on the bus or climb the steps to enter the building is that they use a wheelchair, or that the reason they can't vote is that they can't see the ballot. In other words, it is assumed that the limits on what they can do are caused solely by the condition of their bodies and not *also* by the narrow assumptions made by nondisabled people when they design buildings and buses and the rest of the physical environment. In a society where nondisability is privileged and defined by the dominant group, what is then viewed as "disability" is routinely assumed to be something that resides solely in the person who has it, thereby making it their problem, if not their fault.

The result of such thinking is that oppression is blamed on the people who suffer most from it, while privilege and those who benefit remain invisible and relatively untouched. And off the hook.

CALL IT SOMETHING ELSE

A more subtle way to deny oppression and privilege is to call them something else, thereby creating the appearance of being in touch with reality without having to do something about it.

Gender inequality, for example, is often described as a charming "battle of the sexes," or as an anthropological curiosity based on the idea that males and females come from different cultures, if not different planets. Deborah Tannen tells us in her popular books on gender and language that the problem is primarily one of communication and misunderstanding. The two genders come from essentially different cultures, she writes, and they get into trouble because they don't know how to interpret each other's talk. In fact, however, they grow up in the same families, attend the same schools, watch television and movies together, and play in the same neighborhoods and schoolyards.

And while gender differences in styles of talk do exist, they are more significant than the differences between, say, Japanese and U.S. styles of talk. The differences are more significant because they serve the purpose of ensuring male privilege and keeping women in an inferior position by reflecting the male-dominated, male-centered, male-identified nature of society. Every time a man interrupts a woman, for example, and she defers by keeping silent, a pattern of male dominance and male centeredness is acted out once again, one of the endless tiny events through which social systems and gender privilege happen. There's nothing cute or charming about it, but acting as if there were is a way to avoid looking at what's really going on.

Avoiding the trouble by renaming it is most prevalent in matters of gender inequality. A major reason is that women and men depend on one another in ways that other groups do not. Most whites don't particularly need people of color, for example, but relationships across gender lines are the backbone of most people's lives. This is especially true for heterosexuals, but no matter what your sexual orientation, everyone has parents, and most people have siblings or friendships that are cross-gender. So, how do we live in such close quarters without confronting the reality—and the discomfort—of the trouble surrounding male privilege? Patriarchal culture provides the answer: to see the world through a thick ideology of images and ideas that mask the reality of gender inequality by turning it into something else in our minds.

Men can find ways to make jokes, for example, about every aspect of gender inequality, from violence against women to sexuality to who gets stuck with cleaning the house or changing the diapers. They can laugh about it in ways that would be unthinkable if the subject were race or anti-Semitism. This isn't because gender oppression is less serious than other forms. In many ways just the opposite is true. Instead, it is because gender inequality runs so deep in our lives and has such serious consequences that we must go to great lengths to make it appear normal and so avoid seeing it for what it is.

IT'S BETTER THIS WAY

The combination of denial and calling privilege and oppression something else often results in the claim that everyone actually prefers things the way they are. Whites, for example, may claim that blacks would rather live among other blacks, reflecting a supposedly natural human tendency to choose the company of "your own kind." In fact, however, research shows clearly that most blacks would prefer to live in integrated neighborhoods. If anyone wants to live "with their own kind," it is whites, who do so by enforcing an extreme level of residential segregation in the United States.

Segregation is also portrayed as a matter of simple economics, that people of color don't live among whites because they can't afford to.

But in fact, it is racism, not income, occupation, or education, that stands in the way of integrated living for most people of color, especially those in the middle class.[5]

The thick ideology that surrounds gender privilege includes all kinds of claims that the status quo is best. Patriarchal culture, for example, is full of messages that women prefer strong men who dominate them and make all the "big" decisions. When a woman says no to sex, she at least means maybe and probably means yes. Women "ask" for all kinds of trouble, especially what's otherwise known as rape, sexual harassment, and being beaten by domestic partners. Male superiority is a natural arrangement dictated by genes and other biological imperatives. Men are naturally breadwinners, and women are naturally suited to having bread won for them and tending to children and keeping the house clean. It doesn't matter how much evidence is weighed against such notions. It doesn't matter how often women complain about male control or how often they insist that no means no. It doesn't matter that women have been major "breadwinners" for virtually all of human history and that staying home and being supported by men is an historical anomaly that doesn't apply to the vast majority of people in the world and never has.

The truth doesn't matter because ideology isn't about truth or accuracy. Rather, its purpose is to support and perpetuate the status quo by making it appear normal and legitimate. In this case, the status quo is privilege, and ideology supports it by getting privileged people off the hook. It supports the all too human tendency to soothe yourself into thinking there's nothing unpleasant or challenging here to deal with, and certainly nothing to do with you. And when someone dares to challenge that comforting reality, it's easy to confuse the bearer of bad news with the bad news itself. When people of color call attention to the divisions caused by white privilege, for example, they're often accused of *creating* those divisions, as if racism isn't a problem unless you talk about it. Talking about privilege rather than privilege itself gets defined as the problem.

Being part of the solution to a trouble that already divides us begins with coming together around the simple truth that we're *all* in trouble and that pretending we aren't only keeps us apart.

IT DOESN'T COUNT IF YOU DON'T MEAN IT

Because U.S. culture encourages us to use an individual-guilt model to explain just about everything that goes wrong, it's easy to confuse intentions with consequences. In other words, if something bad happens, someone's conscious bad intentions must be behind it. A corollary is that if your intentions are good, they cannot result in something bad.

As we saw earlier, for example, white racism is usually defined as a bad attitude toward people of color, as malicious intentions buttressed by negative cultural stereotypes. When whites are confronted with matters of race, they usually react as if the issue isn't patterns of inequality and unnecessary suffering but their own personal feelings and views about race and the question of their individual guilt or innocence. They respond as if the challenge is to get themselves off the hook by showing themselves to be pure on the subject of race. They seem to think that if they don't *mean* it, then it didn't happen, as if their conscious intent is the only thing that connects them to the consequences of what they do or don't do.

"I didn't mean it" can stop a conversation before people get to the reality that it doesn't matter whether it was meant or not. The consequence remains the same. Take the case of a white female professor who calls on only whites in class. Since she has no conscious animosity toward people of color, she doesn't see herself as having anything to do with the continuing pattern of racial inequality that results from the choices she makes as she does her job. In other words, she doesn't see herself as part of the problem or, therefore, as part of the solution.

Or a man makes repeated sexual comments to a female colleague. When she gets angry and tells him to stop, he gets defensive. He says it was only a joke, or that he just finds her attractive and meant no harm by it. What he doesn't do is acknowledge that regardless of the intentions he's aware of, he *has* done her harm, and she's likely to be left to deal with it on her own. He acts as though a lack of conscious intent means a lack of effect, as if *saying* it was only a joke or only being *aware* of it as a joke is enough to *make* it just a joke.

Sometimes this insight can take us into unexpected places when we apply it to the mundane details of everyday life. A while ago, for example, a middle-aged man at a talk I gave expressed frustration and concern about whether to open doors for women. "The rules are changing," he said. "I always thought it was the polite thing to do, but now women get mad at me sometimes."

This incident reminded me of an online discussion that began when a woman pointed out that she didn't like it when men rushed ahead to open a door for her to pass through without having to open it herself. "I remember," she wrote, "when I first realized how stupid I felt sitting in a car while a man scurried around to open the door for me." She objected to this "door-opening ceremony" because "it seemed to do more for men than it did for women." She explained that it puts men in a position of control and independence (men can open doors for themselves) and leaves her waiting helplessly for men to do what she could do for herself. Like all rituals, opening doors is symbolic, and it conveys a cultural message that men are active, capable, and independent, whereas women are passive, incapable, and dependent—yet another way to keep men in control.

The men roared back in a defensive chorus. "We aren't *trying* to dominate anyone," wrote one. "We're just being *polite*."

"But," another woman objected, "there's more going on than the men admit." She pointed out that if this ritual were just performed out of politeness, *women* would also feel obliged to open doors for *men*, since being polite is something that runs both ways. Politeness, of course, can go in just one direction, as when subordinates defer to superiors.

"Well, maybe that's what door opening is," a man shot back. "Men are like servants waiting on women."

"But," came the reply, "if that were so, why is it so hard to get men to help us when we really need it? Why are we always stuck with the scut work at home and at work?"

It went on this way for quite a while, women objecting to *consequences* they didn't like and men defending against conscious *intentions* they didn't feel they had. The key to getting unstuck, I think, is to realize that consequences matter whether or not they're matched by intentions. "The road to Hell," as the old saying goes, "is paved with good intentions." When men defend opening doors for women as just being polite, they assume it can't mean something they don't know about.

But what things mean isn't a private matter, because meaning comes from culture. Men can *think* they're just being nice guys, but that doesn't mean rushing ahead to open that door won't have social consequences beyond what they're aware of. In a patriarchal society, there's a good chance that the forms people follow—including being "polite"—are also patriarchal. In short, both sides of the argument can be right: men may not consciously intend to put women down, and what men do often *does* put women down.

It's also worth noting that I didn't get the sense that the women in this conversation were trying to get the men to confess to some evil motive. They weren't trying to make them feel bad about themselves or even apologize. What they wanted was for men to be conscious of what they were doing, to see how such patterns can produce bad consequences, and to do something to stop it.

Toward that end, it is generally useful to ask ourselves what we mean whenever we say, "I didn't mean it," because on some level, it's reasonable to assume that we mean everything we do and say. At a retirement party for a black manager, for example, a white colleague arranged a slide show that included pictures of black people happily eating watermelon, an image with a long history of being used to stereotype blacks as lazy and not smart enough to care about anything more complex than having something sweet to eat. Blacks in the audience were shocked and angered, and when someone confronted the white man later on, his reaction was, "I'm not racist. I didn't mean anything by it."

In effect, "I didn't mean it" often comes close to "I didn't say it" or "I didn't do it," which of course isn't true. What, then, do the words signify? Most of the time, the real message is "I did it, I said it, but I didn't think about it." In many social situations, that kind of response clearly won't work. If I steal someone's car, the judge is unlikely to go easy on me if I say, "I didn't mean anything by it. I just wanted the car and I didn't think much about it at the time." Or, "I didn't consider whether the owner would mind" or "Getting arrested didn't cross my mind." The judge would probably say, "You *should* have thought about it." In other words, I'm held responsible to act with an ongoing awareness of the consequences of what I do and don't do.

But privilege works against such awareness in all kinds of social situations. The manager should have been mindful of racial patterns in mentoring and promotion. The white colleague should have thought about the cultural message behind demeaning stereotypes that associate blacks with watermelon. The man who sexually harassed should have been aware of what it's like to be a woman on the receiving end of such behavior. But they weren't, and such patterns are the norm, not the exception. Why?

If we use an individualistic model of the world, the answer is that people are callous or uncaring or prejudiced or too busy to bother with paying attention to their actions—especially if they're white or heterosexual or male. Sometimes, of course, this is true, but more often the larger truth is that the luxury of obliviousness makes a lack of conscious intent a path of least resistance that's easy to follow without knowing it. The sense of entitlement and superiority that underlies most forms of privilege runs so deep and is so entrenched that people don't have to think about it in order to act from it. They can always say they didn't mean it and, in a real sense, they're telling the truth. That's why "I didn't mean it" can be so disarming and such an effective way to defend privilege. They *weren't* thinking, they *weren't* mindful, they *weren't* aware—all the things that go into "meaning it." But this is precisely the problem with privilege and the damage that it does.

I'M ONE OF THE GOOD ONES

One way to acknowledge the problem of privilege and oppression and get off the hook at the same time is to make use of an illusion we looked at earlier—that bad things happen in social life simply because of bad people. Since I can make a good case that I'm not a bad person, then the trouble couldn't have anything to do with me.

"Racism still exists," I can say, "and it's a shame there are still bigots around like the Klan and skinheads and neo-Nazis." Or, "Unfortunately, some men still haven't gotten used to women in the workplace." Or, "People who haven't worked through their homophobia make life difficult for gays and lesbians."

"And," I can hasten to add, if only to myself, "I don't belong to the Klan, I don't see color, I like women, and I have no 'problem' with gays and lesbians as far as I know, and I never park in those handicapped spaces."

Having set myself up as a good person with good intentions, I can feel disapproval or even compassion for all those bad, flawed, or sick people who supposedly make trouble happen all by themselves in spite of people like me. And I can sympathize with people who suffer as a result. But the issue of just where *I* am in all of this drops out of sight. Apparently I'm on the outside looking in as a concerned observer. I might even have moments when I count myself as a victim, since I feel bad whenever I think about it.

But the truth is that my silence, my inaction, and especially my passive acceptance of the everyday privilege that goes along with group membership are all it takes to make me just as much a part of the problem as any member of the Klan.

It's a point that's easy to miss, because we want people to see and judge us as individuals, not as members of a social category.[6] But when we insist on that, we're being naïve if not somewhat false, for the fact is that we *do* want people to treat us as members of social categories whenever it works to our advantage. When I go into a store, for example, I want to be waited on right away and treated with respect even though the clerks don't know a thing about me as an individual. I want them to accept my check or credit card and not treat me with suspicion and distrust. But all they know about me is the categories they think I belong to—a customer of a certain race, age, gender, disability status, and class—and all the things they think they know about people who belong to those categories. I want that to be enough. I don't want to have to prove over and over again that I'm someone who deserves to be trusted and taken seriously. I want them to *assume* all that, and the only way they can do that is to perceive me as belonging to the "right" social categories.

This is simply how social life works. By itself, it's not a problem. What many people resist seeing, however, is that on the other side of that same social process are all the people who get put into the "wrong" categories and ignored or followed around or treated with suspicion and disrespect regardless of who they are as individuals.

I can't have it both ways. If I'm going to welcome the way social categories work to my advantage, I also have to consider that when those same categories are used against others through no fault of their own, it then becomes *my* business because through that process *I* am being privileged at *their* expense.

In 1990, ABC News aired as a segment of *Prime Time* a documentary called *True Colors* that powerfully illustrates this dynamic. It focused on two men who were quite similar in every observable characteristic except race: one was black and one was white. The crew used hidden cameras and microphones to record what happened in various situations—applying for a job, accidentally locking oneself out of the car, trying to rent an apartment, shopping for shoes, buying a car, and so on. Over and over again the two men were treated differently. In one instance, for example, the white man wandered into a shoe store in a shopping mall. He was barely across the threshold when the white clerk approached him with a smile and an outstretched hand. He looked at some shoes and then went on his way. Minutes later his black partner entered the store and from the outset was utterly ignored by the clerk, who stood only a few feet away. Nothing the black man did seemed to make a difference. He picked up and looked at shoes, he walked up and down the display aisles, he gazed thoughtfully at a particular style. After what seemed an eternity, he left.

When I show *True Colors* in my race class and at diversity training sessions, I ask whites if they identify with anyone in the video. Invariably they say no, because they don't see themselves in the black man's predicament or in the racist behavior of the whites. Somehow, the white partner who is on the receiving end of preferential treatment is invisible to them, and if I don't mention him, he rarely comes up. In other words, they don't say, "Yes, I see myself in the white guy receiving the benefits of white privilege."

The effect of this obliviousness is for *them* to become invisible as white people in everyday situations and unaware of how privilege happens to them, especially in relation to other whites. They don't see themselves as being involved in situations in which privilege comes into play. They don't see, for example, that simply being white puts them in a particular relationship with someone like the shoe store clerk (whom they readily identify as racist) or that this relationship affects the way customers of color are treated and the way *they* are treated as whites.

The invisibility of whiteness illustrates how privilege can blind those who receive it to what's going on. As Ruth Frankenberg writes about a white woman she interviewed, "Beth was much more sharply aware of racial *oppression* shaping Black experience than of race *privilege* shaping her own life. Thus, Beth could be alert to the realities of economic discrimination against Black communities while still conceptualizing her own life as racially neutral—nonracialized, nonpolitical."[7]

A common form of blindness to privilege is that women and people of color are often described as being treated unequally, but men and whites are not. This, however, is logically impossible. *Unequal* simply means "not equal," which describes both those who receive less than their fair share *and* those who receive more. But there can't be a short end of the stick without a long end, because it's the longness of the long end that makes the short end short. To pretend otherwise makes privilege and those who receive it invisible.

So long as we participate in a society that transforms difference into privilege, there is no neutral ground on which to stand. If I'm in a meeting in which men pay more attention to what I and other men say than they do to women, for example, I'm on the receiving end of privilege. My mere acceptance of that privilege—whether conscious or not—is all that other men need from me to perpetuate it. Other men *need* my compliance for male privilege to work, even if my compliance is unconscious and passive. I know this because as soon as I resist that path by speaking out and merely calling attention to it, I can feel the defensive response rise up to meet me. In this sense, I don't have to be consciously hostile toward women in order to play an integral role in maintaining male privilege as a pattern in this society.

In the same way, for white privilege to work, whites need the compliance of other whites. If I look around my workplace and see no people of color, my silence on this issue sends the message to other whites that there *is* no issue. The shoe clerk's racist behavior depends on his being able to assume that other whites don't see a problem with preferential treatment for whites. That's what makes this path of racial preference a path of least resistance. And every white person either supports or challenges that assumption in choosing which path to follow. It is in the nature of social life that people continually look to one another to confirm or deny what they experience as reality. Given that, other people will interpret my going along with them down this path as my acceptance of that path unless I do something to make them think otherwise. Whether we know it or not, when someone discriminates by treating me better simply because I'm white, we walk down a path of white privilege *together.*

There is no such thing as doing nothing. There is no such thing as being neutral or uninvolved. At every moment, social life involves all of us.

SICK AND TIRED

It's not unusual for whites to comment on how sick and tired they are of hearing about race. "It's always in your face," they say. I ask how often is "always," and what does "it" consist of? They become a bit vague. "Oh, it's in the news," they say, "all the time."

"Every day?" I ask.

"Well, it seems like it," they say.

"Every hour, every minute?"

"No, of course not," they say, and I can tell they're starting to get a little irritated with me. I realize they aren't trying to report an objective reality in the world. They're describing the feeling of being annoyed by something, put upon. When you're annoyed by something, it can seem as though it's everywhere, as if there's no escaping it. When it comes to the problem of privilege and oppression, privileged groups don't want to hear about it at *all* because it disturbs the luxury of obliviousness that comes with privilege. This means you don't have to bring it up often for them to feel put upon. "Always" turns out to be somewhere between never and every minute. In reality, "all the time" comes down to "enough to make me look at what I don't want to look at, enough to make me uncomfortable." And usually that doesn't take much.

A similar dynamic operates with most forms of privilege. The middle and upper classes say they're sick and tired of hearing about welfare and poverty. Nondisabled people are sick and tired of hearing about disability issues. And it takes almost no criticism at all for members of dominant groups to feel "bashed," as if it's "open season on us." In fact, just saying something like "male privilege" or "patriarchy" can start eyes rolling and evoke that exasperated sense of "Here we go *again.*"

In fact, however, there is almost always utter silence in this society on the subject of male privilege. In a system that privileges maleness, the default is *never* to do anything that might make *men* feel challenged or uncomfortable as men. In the same way, because whiteness is privileged over color, the norm is to never call attention to whiteness itself in ways that make white people uncomfortable. It's expected, of course, to routinely draw attention to male and white and nondisabled and heterosexual *people,* since our society is centered on and identified with those groups. But that differs from drawing attention to "male," "heterosexual," "nondisabled," or "white" as social categories that are problematic.

Another reason for the "sick and tired" complaint is that life is hard for everyone. "Don't bring us your troubles," privileged groups say to the rest, "we've got troubles of our own." Many white men, for example, especially those who lack class privilege, spend a lot of time worrying about losing their jobs. So, why should they have to listen to women or people of color talk about problems with work, especially when the talk suggests that white men should be doing something more than they already are? When Marian Wright Edelman, founder and president of the Children's Defense Fund, says that it's "utterly exhausting being Black in America," many white people barely miss a beat in responding that they're tired, too.[8]

And of course, they are. They're exhausted from the pace of life that a competitive capitalist society imposes on everyone, and it's hard to hear about privilege and oppression. But it's one thing to have to hear about such problems and another to have to live them every day. The quick white defensiveness runs right past the fact that whatever it is that exhausts white people, it isn't the fact of being white. It may be exhausting to be a parent or a worker or a spouse or a student who works all day and studies all night, but it's not exhausting to be a white person or, for that matter, a heterosexual or a man.

By comparison, people in subordinate groups have to do all the things that also exhaust members of dominant groups, from raising families to earning a living to getting older. But on top of that, they must also struggle with the accumulation of fine grinding grit that oppression loads onto people's lives simply because they're in the "wrong" social category.

"I'm sick and tired" is a defense that allows privileged groups to claim the protected status of victims. It reminds me of those times when people injure you in some way, and when you confront them about it, they get angry at *you* because you've made them feel guilty about what they did. "Look how bad you've made me feel," they say, as if you're supposed to apologize for bringing your injury to their attention. Children often use this defense because they're so self-centered that the idea of taking responsibility for what they've done doesn't occur to them. When confronted with their misbehavior they may sulk and glower and act hurt and put upon, as if someone has just laid a heavy and undeserved weight on their shoulders.

Privilege similarly encourages people to be self-centered and unaccountable to others. It encourages whites and men and other advantaged groups to behave as less than adults. It makes avoiding responsibility for what they do and don't do a path of least resistance. And yet, at the same time, these are the groups in charge of social institutions. People in these groups are the ones who occupy positions of responsible adult authority. It's a combination guaranteed to keep privilege and oppression going unless the cycle of denial and defense is broken. The challenge for dominant groups is to see how privilege keeps them from growing up, how it diminishes everyone—including them—and blocks their potential to be part of the solution.

GETTING OFF THE HOOK BY GETTING ON

If being on the hook for privilege and oppression means being perpetually vulnerable to guilt and blame, then we shouldn't be surprised that people do whatever they can to get off it. But according to my dictionary, *on the hook* also means being "committed," "obliged," and "involved."

In this sense, being on the hook is one of those things that distinguish adults from children—adults are and children aren't. When I'm on the hook, I feel called on to use my power and authority as an adult to take responsibility, to act, to make things happen. Being "involved" makes me part of something larger, and I can't stand alone as an isolated individual. Being "obliged" means more than just being burdened, because it also connects me to people and makes me aware of how I affect them. And being "committed" to something focuses my potential to make a difference and bonds me to those who feel the same way.

Off the hook, I'm like a piece of wood floating with the current. On the hook, I have forward motion and a rudder to steer by. Off the hook, I live in illusion and denial, as if I can choose whether to be involved in the life of our society and the consequences it produces. But involvement is something that comes with being alive in the world as a human being. On the hook is where I can live fully in the world as it really is.

Trying to live off the hook puts members of privileged groups inside a tight little circle that cuts them off from much of what it means to be alive. They have to work to distance themselves from most of humanity, because they can't get close to other people without touching the trouble that surrounds privilege and oppression. Men living off the hook distance and insulate themselves from women, whites from people of color, heterosexuals from lesbians and gay men, the nondisabled from those with disabilities, the middle and upper classes from the working and lower classes. And the more diverse and interconnected the world becomes, the harder it is to sustain the illusion and the denial day after day, the more it takes to maintain the distance and deny the connection. The result of illusion and denial is to become like the person who loses the ability to feel pain and risks bleeding to death from a thousand tiny cuts that go unnoticed, untreated, and unhealed.

Sooner or later, dominant groups must embrace this hook they're on, not as some terrible affliction or occasion for guilt and shame but as a challenge and an opportunity. It's where they've been, where they are, and where they're going.

CHAPTER 9

What Can We Do?

The challenge we face is to change patterns of exclusion, rejection, privilege, harassment, discrimination, and violence that are everywhere in this society and have existed for hundreds (or, in the case of gender, thousands) of years. We have to begin by thinking about the trouble and the challenge in new and more productive ways as outlined in the preceding chapters. Here is a summary of the tools we've identified so far.

Large numbers of people have sat on the sidelines and seen themselves as part of neither the problem nor the solution. Beyond this, however, they are far from homogeneous. Everyone is aware of people who intentionally act out in oppressive ways. But there is less attention given to the millions of people who know inequities exist and want to be part of the solution. Their silence and invisibility allow privilege and oppression to continue. Removing what silences them and stands in their way can tap an enormous potential of energy for change.

The problem of privilege and oppression is deep and wide, and to work with it we have to be able to see it clearly so that we can talk about it in useful ways. To do that, we have to reclaim some difficult language that names what's going on, language that has been so misused and maligned that it generates more heat than light. We can't just stop using words like *racism, sexism, ableism,* and *privilege,* however, because these are tools that focus our awareness on the problem and all the forms it takes. Once we can see and talk about what's going on, we can analyze how it works as a system. We can identify points of leverage where change can begin.

Reclaiming the language takes us directly to the core reality that the problem is privilege and the power that maintains it. Privilege exists when one group has something that is systematically denied to others not because of who they are or what they've done or not done but because of the social category they belong to. Privilege is a feature of social systems, not individuals. People have or don't have privilege depending on the system they're in and the social categories other people put them in.

In dealing with the problem of privilege, we have to get used to being surrounded by paradox, such as those having privilege not knowing it. Also paradoxical is the fact that privilege doesn't necessarily lead to a "good life," which can prompt people in privileged groups to deny resentfully that they even have it.

For several centuries, capitalism has provided the economic context for privilege and oppression. As such, it has been and continues to be a powerful force, especially in relation to class, gender, and race. Its effects are both direct and indirect. Historically, it was the engine that drove the development of modern racism. In a less direct way, it creates conditions of scarcity that set the stage for competition, fear, and antagonism directed across differences of race, ethnicity, and gender. Through the class differences that it creates, it also shapes people's experience of privilege and the lack of it. This is an example of the matrix of domination (or matrix of privilege) through which the various forms of difference and privilege interact and shape one another.

Difference takes many forms, but the most important are those characteristics that are difficult or impossible to change and that other people think they can identify just by looking at someone. Oppression also takes many forms, most notably avoidance, exclusion, rejection, unequal access to resources and rewards, and violence. Just as privileged groups tend not to be aware of privilege, they also tend not to be aware of how it happens from one moment to the next.

Although disadvantaged groups take the brunt of the trouble, privileged groups are also affected by it, partly because misery visited on others comes back to haunt those who benefit from it, especially in the form of defensiveness and fear. But trouble also affects privileged groups directly by limiting and shaping the lives of people who have privilege. The trouble also affects entire social systems, from families to corporations and schools to communities, societies, and global political and economic systems.

The greatest barrier to change is that dominant groups, as we've discussed, don't see the trouble as *their* trouble, which means they don't feel obliged to do something about it. This happens for a variety of reasons—because they don't know the trouble exists in the first place, because they don't *have* to see it as their trouble, because they see it as a personal rather than a systemic problem, because they're reluctant to give up privilege, because they feel angry and deprived and closed to the idea that they have privilege, because they're blinded by prejudice, because they're afraid of what will happen if they acknowledge the reality of privilege and oppression.

The two main approaches to change in organizations do little about these barriers. The "tin cup" approach and "business case" argument aren't powerful enough to engage members of dominant groups over the long haul required for change. Those choices are the horns of the diversity dilemma on which most organizations find themselves today.

A third choice is to think about the trouble as everyone's responsibility—everybody's "hook"—and nobody's fault. This is especially useful for members of privileged groups who have a hard time seeing themselves in relation to privilege without feeling guilty. It's easy to fall into this trap because people tend to use an individualistic model of the world that reduces everything to individual intentions and goodness or badness. A powerful and liberating alternative comes from the fact that we're always participating in something larger than ourselves, social systems. To understand privilege and oppression, we have to look at what we're participating in *and* how we participate in relation to paths of least resistance. This means we can be involved in a society's or organization's troubles without doing anything wrong and without being bad people.

Privilege is created and maintained through social systems that are dominated by, centered on, and identified with privileged groups. A racist society, for example, is white-dominated, white-centered, and white-identified. Since privilege is rooted primarily in systems—such as families, schools, and workplaces—change isn't simply a matter of changing people. The solution also has to include entire systems whose paths of least resistance shape how people feel, think, and behave as individuals, how they see themselves and one another.

As they work for change, it's easy for members of privileged groups to lose sight of the reality of privilege and its consequences and the truth that the trouble surrounding privilege is their trouble as much as anyone else's. This happens in large part because systems of privilege provide endless ways of seeing and thinking about the world that make privilege invisible. As we have seen, these include denying and minimizing the trouble, blaming the victim, calling the trouble something else, assuming everyone prefers things the way they are, mistaking intentions with consequences, attributing the trouble to others and not their own participation in social systems that produce it, and balancing the trouble with troubles of their own. The more aware people can be of how all of this limits their effectiveness, the more they can contribute to change both in themselves and in the systems where they work and live.

With this approach, we can begin to think about how to make ourselves part of the solution to the problem of privilege and oppression. To do that, we first have to deal with some powerful myths about how change happens and how people contribute to it.

MYTH 1: "IT'S ALWAYS BEEN THIS WAY, AND IT ALWAYS WILL"

If you don't make a point of studying history, it's easy to slide into the belief that things have always been the way we've known them to be. But if you look back, you find that white privilege has been a feature of human life for only a matter of centuries, and there is abundant evidence that male privilege has been around for only seven thousand years or so, which isn't very long when you consider that human beings have been on the earth for hundreds of thousands of years.[1] So, when it comes to human social life, the smart money should be on the idea that *nothing* has always been this way or any other.

This idea should suggest that nothing *will* always be this way or any other, contrary to the notion that privilege and oppression are here to stay. If the only thing we can count on is change, then it's hard to see why we should believe for a minute that *any* kind of social system is permanent. Reality is always in motion. Things may appear to stand still, but that's only because humans have a short attention span, dictated perhaps by the relative shortness of our lives. If we take the long view—the *really* long view—we can see that everything is in process all the time.

Some would argue that everything *is* process, the space between one point and another, the movement from one thing toward another. What we may see as permanent end points—world capitalism, Western civilization, advanced technology, and so on—are actually temporary states on the way to other temporary states. Even ecologists, who used to talk about ecological balance, now speak of ecosystems as inherently unstable. Instead of always returning to some steady state after a period of disruption, ecosystems are, by nature, a continuing process of change from one arrangement to another. They never go back to just where they were.

Social systems are also fluid. A society isn't some hulking *thing* that sits there forever as it is. Because a system happens only as people participate in it, it can't help being a dynamic process of creation and re-creation from one moment to the next. In something as simple as a man following the path of least resistance toward controlling conversations (and a woman letting him do it), the reality of male privilege in that moment comes into being. This is how we *do* male privilege, bit by bit, moment by moment. This is also how individuals can contribute to change: by choosing paths of *greater* resistance, as when men don't take control and women refuse their own subordination.

Since people can always choose paths of greater resistance or create new ones entirely, systems can only be as stable as the flow of human choice and creativity, which certainly isn't a recipe for permanence. In the short run, systems of privilege may look unchangeable. But the relentless process of social life never produces the exact same result twice in a row, because it's impossible for everyone to participate in any system in an unvarying and uniform way. Added to this are the dynamic interactions that go on among systems—between capitalism and the state, for example, or between families and the economy—that also produce powerful and unavoidable tensions, contradictions, and other currents of change. Ultimately, systems change because they can't help it.

An oppressive system often *seems* stable because it limits people's lives and imaginations so much that they can't see beyond the limitations. This is especially true when a social system has existed for so long that its past extends beyond collective memory of anything different. As a result, it lays down terms of social life—including various forms of privilege—that can easily be mistaken for some kind of normal and inevitable human condition.

But this situation masks a fundamental long-term instability caused by the dynamics of oppression itself. Any system organized around one group's efforts to control and exploit another is ultimately a losing proposition, because it contradicts the essentially uncontrollable nature of reality and does violence to basic human needs and values. For example, as the last two centuries of feminist thought and action have begun to challenge the violence and break down the denial, patriarchy has become increasingly vulnerable. This is one reason male resistance, backlash, and defensiveness are now so intense. Many men complain about their lot, especially their inability to realize ideals of control in relation to their own lives,[2] women, and other men. Fear of and resentment toward women are pervasive, from worrying about being accused of sexual harassment to railing against affirmative action.

No social system lasts forever, and this fact holds especially for oppressive systems of privilege. We can't know what will replace existing social systems, but we can be confident that they will go, that they *are* going at every moment. It's only a matter of how quickly, by what means, and toward what alternatives, and whether each of us will do our part to make change happen sooner rather than later and with less rather than more human suffering in the process.

MYTH 2: GANDHI'S PARADOX
AND THE MYTH OF NO EFFECT

Whether we help change systems of privilege depends on how we handle the belief that nothing we do can make a difference, that the system is too big and powerful for us to affect. The complaint is valid if we look at society as a whole, because we aren't going to change it in our lifetime. But if changing the entire system through our own efforts is the standard against which we measure the ability to do something, then we've set ourselves up to feel powerless. It's not unreasonable to want to make a difference, but if we have to *see* the final result of what we do, then we can't be part of change that's too gradual and long term to allow that. We also can't be part of change that's so complex that we can't sort out our contribution from countless others that combine in ways we can never grasp. The problem of privilege and oppression requires complex and long-term change coupled with short-term work to soften some of its worst consequences. This means that if we're going to be part of the solution, we have to let go of the idea that change doesn't happen unless we're around to see it.

To shake off the paralyzing myth that we cannot, individually, be effective, we have to alter how we see ourselves in relation to a long-term, complex process of change. This begins by altering how we relate to time. Many changes can come about quickly enough for us to see them happen. When I was in college, for example, there was little talk about gender inequality as a social problem, whereas now there are more than five hundred women's studies programs in the United States. But a goal such as ending privilege takes more than this and far more time than our short lives can encompass. If we're going to see ourselves as part of that kind of change, we can't use the human life span as a significant standard against which to measure progress.

To see our choices in relation to long-term change, we have to develop what might be called "time constancy," analogous to what psychologists call "object constancy." If you hold a cookie in front of very young children and then put it behind your back while they watch, they can't find the cookie because they apparently can't hold on to the image of it and where it went. They lack object constancy. In other words, if they can't see it, it might as well not even exist. After a while, children develop the mental ability to know that objects or people exist even when they're out of sight. In thinking about change and our relation to it, we need to develop a similar ability in relation to time that enables us to carry within us the knowledge, the faith, that significant change happens even though we aren't around to see it.

Along with time constancy, we need to clarify for ourselves how our choices matter and how they don't. Gandhi once said that nothing we do as individuals matters but that it's vitally important to do it anyway. This touches on a powerful paradox in the relationship between society and individuals. Imagine, for example, that social systems are trees and we are the leaves. No individual leaf on the tree matters; whether it lives or dies has no effect on much of anything. But collectively, the leaves are essential to the whole tree because they photosynthesize the sugar that feeds it. Without leaves, the tree dies.

So leaves matter and they don't, just as we matter and we don't. What each of us does may not seem like much, because in important ways, it *isn't* much. But when many people do this work together they can form a critical mass that is anything but insignificant, especially in the long run. If we're going to be part of a larger change process, we have to learn to live with this sometimes uncomfortable paradox.

A related paradox is that we have to be willing to travel without knowing where we're going. We need faith to do what seems right without necessarily being sure of the effect that will have. We have to think like pioneers who may know the direction they want to move in or what they would like to find, without knowing where they will wind up. Because they are going where they've never been before, they can't know whether they will ever arrive at anything they might consider a destination, much less the kind of place they had in mind when they first set out. If pioneers had to know their destination from the beginning, they might never go anywhere or discover anything.

In similar ways, to seek out alternatives to systems of privilege, we have to move away from social life organized around privilege and oppression and move toward the certainty that alternatives are possible, even though we may not have a clear idea of what those are or ever experience them. It has to be enough to question how we see ourselves as people of a certain race, gender, sexual orientation, disability status, and class, or examine how we see capitalism and the scarcity and competition it produces in relation to our personal striving to better our own lives, or look at how privilege and oppression work and how we participate. Then we can open ourselves to experience what happens next.

When we dare ask core questions about who we are and how the world works, things happen that we can't foresee. But they don't happen unless we *move*, if only in our minds. As pioneers, we discover what's possible only by first putting ourselves in motion, because we have to move in order to change our position—and hence our perspective—on where we are, where we've been, and where we might go. This is how alternatives begin to appear.

The myth of no effect obscures the role we can play in the long-term transformation of society. But the myth also blinds us to our own power in relation to other people. We may cling to the belief that there is nothing we can do precisely because we subconsciously know how much power we *do* have and are afraid to use it because people may not like it. If we deny our power to affect people, then we don't have to worry about taking responsibility for how we use it or, more significant, how we don't.

This reluctance to acknowledge and use power comes up in the simplest everyday situations, as when a group of friends starts laughing at a racist or sexist joke and you have to decide whether to go along. It's just a moment among countless such moments that constitute the fabric of all kinds of oppressive systems. But it's a crucial moment, because the group's seamless response to the joke affirms the normalcy and unproblematic nature of it in a system of privilege. It takes only one person to tear the fabric of collusion and apparent consensus. On some level, each of us knows that we have this potential, and this knowledge can empower us or scare us into silence. We can change the course of the moment with something as simple as visibly not joining in the laughter, or saying "I don't think that's funny." We know how uncomfortable this can make the group feel and how they may ward off their discomfort by dismissing, excluding, or even attacking us as bearers of bad news. Our silence, then, isn't because nothing we do will matter. Our silence is our not *daring* to matter.

Our power to affect other people isn't simply the power to make them feel uncomfortable. Systems shape the choices people make primarily by providing paths of least resistance. Whenever we openly choose a different path, however, we make it possible for others to see both the path of least resistance they're following and the possibility of choosing something else.

If we choose different paths, we usually won't know if we're affecting other people, but it's safe to assume that we are. When people know that alternatives exist and witness other people choosing them, things become possible that weren't before. When we openly pass up a path of least resistance, we increase resistance for other people around that path, because now they must reconcile their choice with what they've seen us do, something they didn't have to deal with before. There's no way to predict how this will play out in the long run, but there's certainly no good reason to think it won't make a difference.

The simple fact is that we affect one another all the time without knowing it. When my family moved to our house in northwestern Connecticut, one of my first pleasures was blazing walking trails through the woods. Some time later I noticed deer scat and hoofprints along the trails, and it pleased me to think they had adopted the trail I'd laid down. But then I wondered if perhaps I had followed a trail laid down by others when I cleared "my" trail. I realized there is no way to know that anything begins or ends with me and the choices I make. It's more likely that the paths others have chosen influence the paths I choose.

This suggests that the simplest way to help others make different choices is to make them myself, and to do it openly. As I shift the patterns of my own participation in systems of privilege, I make it easier for others to do so as well, and harder for them not to. Simply by setting an example—rather than trying to change them—I create the possibility of their participating in change in their own time and in their own way. In this way I can widen the circle of change without provoking the kind of defensiveness that perpetuates paths of least resistance and the oppressive systems they serve.

It's important to see that in doing this kind of work, we don't have to go after people to change their minds. In fact, changing people's minds may play a relatively small part in changing systems. We won't succeed in turning diehard misogynists into practicing feminists, for example, or racists into civil rights activists. At most, we can shift the odds in favor of new paths that contradict the core values that systems of privilege depend on. We can introduce so many exceptions to the paths that support privilege that the children or grandchildren of diehard racists and misogynists will start to change their perception of which paths offer the least resistance. Research on men's changing attitudes toward the male provider role, for example, shows that most of the shift occurs *between* generations, not within them.[3] This suggests that rather than trying to change people, the most important thing we can do is contribute to shifting entire cultures so that forms and values that support privilege begin to lose their "obvious" legitimacy and normalcy, and new forms emerge to challenge their privileged place in social life. And when this happens, the structures of privilege— segregation and the unequal and oppressive distribution of wealth, power, resources, and opportunities—become harder to maintain.

In science, this is how one paradigm replaces another.[4] For hundreds of years, for example, Europeans believed that stars, planets, and the sun revolved around Earth. But Copernicus and Galileo found that too many of their astronomical observations were anomalies that didn't fit the prevailing paradigm: if the sun and planets revolved around Earth, then they wouldn't move as they did. As such observations accumulated, they made it increasingly difficult to hang on to an Earth-centered paradigm. Eventually the anomalies became so numerous that Copernicus offered a new paradigm, which he declined to publish for fear of persecution as a heretic, a fate that eventually befell Galileo when he took up the cause a century later. Eventually, however, the evidence was so overwhelming that a new paradigm replaced the old one.

In similar ways, we can see how systems of privilege are based on paradigms that shape how we think about difference and how we organize social life in relation to it. We can openly challenge those paradigms with evidence that they don't work and produce unacceptable consequences for everyone. We can help weaken them by openly choosing alternative paths in our everyday lives and thereby provide living anomalies that don't fit the prevailing paradigm. By our example, we can contradict basic assumptions and their legitimacy over and over again. We can add our choices and our lives to tip the scales toward new paradigms that don't revolve around privilege and oppression. We can't tip the scales overnight or by ourselves, and in that sense we don't amount to much. But, as Gandhi noted, it is crucial where we choose to place what poet Bonaro Overstreet called "the stubborn ounces of my weight":

STUBBORN OUNCES

(To One Who Doubts the Worth of Doing Anything
If You Can't Do Everything)

You say the little efforts that I make
will do no good; they will never prevail
to tip the hovering scale
where Justice hangs in balance.
                              I don't think
I ever thought they would.
But I am prejudiced beyond debate
In favor of my right to choose which side
shall feel the stubborn ounces of my weight.[5]

It is in small and humble choices that privilege, oppression, and the movement toward something better actually happen.

STUBBORN OUNCES: WHAT CAN WE DO?

There are no easy answers to the question of what can we do about the problem of privilege. There is no twelve-step program, no neat set of instructions. Most important, there is no way around or over it: the only way out is through it. We won't end oppression by pretending it isn't there or that we don't have to deal with it.

Some people complain that those who work for social change are being "divisive" when they draw attention to oppressive systems organized around one form of privilege or another. But when members of dominant groups mark differences by excluding or discriminating against subordinate groups and treating them as "other," they aren't accused of being divisive. Usually it's only when someone calls attention to how differences are used as a basis for privilege that the charge of divisiveness comes up.

In a sense, it *is* divisive to say that privilege exists, but only insofar as it points to divisions that already exist and to the perception that the status quo is normal and unremarkable. Privilege promotes the worst kind of divisiveness because it cuts us off from one another and, by silencing us about the truth, cuts us off from ourselves as well. Not only must we participate in privilege and oppression by living in this society, we also must act as though they don't exist, denying the reality of our own experience and its consequences for people's lives, including our own.

What does it mean to go out by going through? What can we do that will make a difference?

Acknowledge That Privilege and Oppression Exists

A key to the continued existence of every system of privilege is unawareness, because privilege contradicts so many basic human values that it invariably arouses opposition when people know about it. The Soviet Union and its East European satellites, for example, were riddled with contradictions so widely known among their people that the oppressive regimes fell apart with an ease and speed that astonished the world. An awareness of privilege and oppression compels people to speak out, to break the silence that any system depends on to continue.

This is why most cultures of privilege mask the reality of oppression by denying its existence, trivializing it, calling it something else, blaming it on those most victimized by it, or diverting attention from it. Instead of treating oppression as a serious problem, we go to war or get embroiled in controversial "issues" such as capital gains tax cuts or "family values" or immigrant workers. There would be far more active opposition to white privilege, for example, if white people lived with an ongoing awareness of how it actually affects the everyday lives of those it oppresses as "not white." As we have seen, however, the vast majority of white people *don't* do this.

It's one thing to become aware and quite another to stay that way. The greatest challenge when we first become aware of a critical perspective on the world is simply to hang on to it. Every system's paths of least resistance invariably lead away from critical awareness of how the system works. In some ways, it's harder and more important to pay attention to systems of privilege than it is to people's behavior and the paths of least resistance that shape it. As we saw earlier, for example, the structure of capitalism creates large social patterns of inequality, scarcity, and exploitation that have played and continue to play a major role in the perpetuation of various forms of privilege and oppression. It is probably wishful thinking to suppose we can end privilege without also changing a capitalist system of political economy that allows an elite to control the vast majority of wealth and income and leaves the rest of the population to fight over what's left. But such wishful thinking is, in fact, what we're encouraged to engage in most of the time—to cling to the idea that racism, for example, is just a problem with a few bad whites, rather than seeing how it is connected to a much larger matrix of privilege and oppression.

By not looking at the institutions through which humans organize economic and social life, we also engage in the fantasy that solving the problem of privilege is only a matter of changing how individual people think. I have, of course, spent most of this book talking about the importance of changing how we think about these issues, and I haven't suddenly changed my mind. We have for a long time been stuck in our ability to deal with these issues, and changing how we think is a key to getting unstuck.

By itself, however, changing how we think won't be enough to solve the problem. Privilege will not simply go away as the result of a change in individual consciousness. Ultimately, we'll have to apply our understanding of how systems work to the job of changing systems themselves—economic, political, religious, educational, and familial. To return to my earlier discussion of the game of Monopoly: we have two choices if we don't like the consequences that result from playing it. One is to do what I did and stop. But since we don't have the option of not participating in our society, we're left with the second choice, which is to change the game.

Since there is a lot of resistance to following such paths, the easiest thing to do after reading a book like this is to forget about it. Maintaining a critical consciousness takes commitment and work. Awareness is something that either we maintain in the moment or we don't. And the only way to hang on to an awareness of privilege is to make that awareness an ongoing part of our lives.

Pay Attention

Understanding how privilege and oppression operate and how you participate is where working for change begins. It's easy to have opinions, but it takes work to know what you're talking about. The simplest way to begin is to make reading about privilege part of your life. Unless you have the luxury of a personal teacher, you can't understand this issue without reading. Many people assume they already know what they need to know because it's part of everyday life. But they're usually wrong, because just as the last thing a fish would discover is water, the last thing people discover is society itself and something as pervasive as privilege.

We also have to be open to the idea that what we think we know is, if not wrong, so deeply shaped by systems of privilege that it misses most of the truth. This is why activists talk with one another and spend time reading one another's writing, because seeing things clearly is tricky. This is also why people who are critical of the status quo are so often self-critical as well—they know how complex and elusive the truth really is and what a challenge it is to work toward it. People working for change are often accused of being orthodox and rigid, but in practice they are typically among the most self-critical people around.

There is a huge literature on issues of privilege available through any decent library system, although you'd never know it to judge from its invisibility in the mass media and mainstream bookstores. For that reason, it's a good idea not to rely on the media for a meaningful analysis. As large capitalist enterprises, the media have a vested interest in ignoring most of what is known about privilege, especially anything that seriously questions the status quo. Instead, they routinely focus on issues that have the least to do with privilege and oppression, that reflect the flawed individualistic models of social life, and that set subordinate groups against one another.

The media would rather discuss whether women and men have different brains, for example, than examine the reality of male privilege. And they are only too happy to give front-page coverage to any woman willing to criticize feminism, or any person of color willing to attack affirmative action or blame other people of color for their disadvantaged position in society. At the same time, the media ignore most of what is known about privilege. Most feminist work, for example, is virtually invisible to book reviewers, journalists, editorial writers, columnists, and the audience for trade books. So, if you want to know what's going on, it may take an interlibrary loan request or a special order at the bookstore. But you can do more. You can also tell librarians and bookstore managers how surprised and disappointed you are that they don't stock such essential reading for understanding the world.

As you educate yourself, avoid reinventing the wheel. Many people have already done a lot of work that you can learn from. There's no way to get through it all, but you don't have to in order to develop a clear enough sense of how to act in meaningful and informed ways. A good place to start is a basic text on race, class, and gender (these books increasingly include discussions of sexual orientation and disability as well; see the Resources section of this book). Men who feel there is no place for them in women's studies might start with books about patriarchy and gender inequality that are written by men. In the same way, whites can begin with writings on race privilege written by other whites. Sooner or later, however, dominant groups will need to turn to what people in subordinate groups have written, because they are the ones who have done most of the work of figuring out how privilege and oppression operate.

Reading is only the beginning. At some point you have to look at yourself and the world to see if you can identify what you're reading about. Once the phrase "paths of least resistance" becomes part of your active vocabulary, for example, you start seeing them all over the place. The more aware you are of how powerful those paths are, the more easily you can decide whether to go down them each time they present themselves.

It helps to live like anthropologists, participant-observers who watch and listen to other people and themselves, who notice patterns that come up again and again in social life. You can pretend you're a stranger in a strange land who knows nothing about where you are and *know* that you know nothing. This approach keeps you open to recognizing faulty assumptions and the surprise of realizing that things aren't what they seem. Following this path is especially challenging for dominant groups, whose privilege tells them they shouldn't have to work to figure out someone else, that it's up to "others" to figure *them* out. It's easy for them to fall into the trap of being like impatient, arrogant tourists who don't take the initiative to educate themselves about where they are. But taking responsibility means not waiting for others to tell you what to do, to point out what's going on, or to identify alternatives. If dominant groups are going to take their share of responsibility, it's up to them to listen, watch, ask, and listen again, to make it their business to find out for themselves. If they don't, they'll slide down the comfortable blindered path of privilege. And then they'll be *just* part of the problem and they *will* be blamed and they'll have it coming.

Learn to Listen[6]

Attentive listening is especially difficult for members of dominant groups. If someone confronts you with your own behavior that supports privilege, step off the path of least resistance that encourages you to defend and deny. Don't tell them they're too sensitive or need a better sense of humor, and don't try to explain away what you did as something else than what they're telling you it was. Don't say you didn't mean it or that you were only kidding. Don't tell them what a champion of justice you are or how hurt you feel because of what they're telling you. Don't make jokes or try to be cute or charming, since only access to privilege can lead someone to believe these are acceptable responses to something as serious as privilege and oppression. Listen to what's being said. Take it seriously. Assume for the time being that it's true, because given the power of paths of least resistance, it probably is. And then take responsibility to do something about it.

A student of color in one of my classes, for example, once told me that she noticed my cutting her off during class, something she didn't think I did with white students. I could have weighed in with my professorial authority and said it wasn't true, that she was imagining it, that I treat all my students that way, that she was being too sensitive, that I travel all over the country speaking about issues of inequality and injustice, so certainly I was above such things. But what I said to her was that I was truly sorry she'd had that experience. I wasn't aware of doing that, I told her, and the fact that I didn't consciously mean to was beside the point.

To respond in this way, I had to de-center myself from my position of privilege and make her experience and not mine the point of the conversation. I ended by telling her I would do everything I could to pay attention to this problem in the future to make sure it didn't happen again.

Note that my goodness or badness as a person was not the issue. The issues were the existence of pervasive racist patterns through which privilege is enacted every day, and the part all of us play in it, and my willingness to take responsibility for paying attention to my own behavior as a participant. I believe that most of the time, members of subordinate groups are not looking for dominant groups to feel ashamed or guilty, because this will do nothing in itself to improve their own lives. In my experience, their true goal is to end privilege and oppression and get dominant groups to commit themselves to doing whatever they can to make that happen.

Little Risks: Do Something

The more you pay attention to privilege and oppression, the more you'll see opportunities to do something about them. You don't have to mount an expedition to find opportunities; they're all over the place, beginning with you. As I became aware of how male privilege encourages me to control conversations, for example, I also realized how easily men dominate group meetings by controlling the agenda and interrupting, without women's objecting to it. This pattern is especially striking in groups that are mostly female but in which most of the talking nonetheless comes from a few men. I would find myself sitting in meetings and suddenly the preponderance of male voices would jump out at me, an unmistakable sign of male privilege in full bloom.

As I've seen what's going on, I've had to decide what to do about this little path of least resistance and my relation to it that leads me to follow it so readily. With some effort, I've tried out new ways of listening more and talking less. At times my methods have felt contrived and artificial, such as telling myself to shut up for a while or even counting slowly to ten (or more) to give others a chance to step into the space afforded by silence. With time and practice, new paths have become easier to follow, and I spend less time monitoring myself. But awareness is never automatic or permanent, because paths of least resistance will be there to choose or not as long as male privilege exists.

You might be thinking at this point that everything comes down to changing individuals after all since doing something is a matter of people's behavior. In a sense, of course, it's true that, for us, it all comes down to what we do or don't do as individuals since that's what we are. But the key is to always connect our choices to the systems we participate in. When you *openly* change how you participate in a system, you do more than change your own behavior; you also change how the system happens. When you change how a system happens, you change the social environment that shapes other people's behavior, which, in turn, further changes how the system happens. And when you do that, you also help to change the consequences that come out of the dynamic relationship between systems and individuals, including patterns of privilege and oppression.

Sometimes stepping off the path of least resistance is a matter of directly calling attention to the system and how it's organized. As you'll see below, for example, it might involve calling attention to the distribution of power and resources in an organization—why are all the secretaries women and all the executives men? Why is the custodial staff mostly people of color and the management staff entirely white? Choosing to call attention to such patterns means changing your own behavior, but it does more than that because the focus of your choice is the system itself.

In short, since the world happens as it does through the dynamic relationship between individuals and social systems, changing the world has to involve both.

As you become more aware, questions will arise about what goes on at work, in the media, in families, in communities, in religious institutions, in government, on the street, and at school—in short, just about everywhere. The questions don't come all at once (for which we can be grateful), although they sometimes come in a rush that can feel overwhelming. If you remind yourself that it isn't up to you to do it all, however, you can see plenty of situations in which you can make a difference, sometimes in surprisingly simple ways. Consider the following possibilities.

Make noise, be seen. Stand up, volunteer, speak out, write letters, sign petitions, show up. Every oppressive system feeds on silence. Don't collude in it. Breaking the silence is especially important for dominant groups, because it undermines the assumption of solidarity that privilege depends on. If this feels too risky, practice being aware of how silence reflects your investment in solidarity with other dominant-group members. This can be a place to begin working on how you participate in making privilege and oppression happen: "Today I said nothing, colluded in silence, and this is how I benefited from it. Tomorrow I can try something different."

Find little ways to withdraw support from paths of least resistance and people's choices to follow them, starting with yourself. It can be as simple as not laughing at a racist or heterosexist joke or saying you don't think it's funny, or writing a letter to your senator or representative or the editor of your newspaper, objecting to an instance of sexism in the media. When my local newspaper ran an article whose headline referred to sexual harassment as "earthy behavior," for example, I wrote a letter pointing out that harassment has nothing to do with being "earthy."

The key to withdrawing support is to interrupt the flow of business as usual. You can subvert the assumption that everyone's going along with the status quo by simply not going along. When you do this, you stop the flow, if only for a moment, but in that moment other people can notice and start to think and question. It's a perfect time to suggest the possibility of alternatives, such as humor that isn't at someone else's expense, or of ways to think about discrimination, harassment, and violence that do justice to the reality of what's going on and how it affects people.

People often like to think of themselves as individuals—especially in the United States. But it's amazing how much of the time we compare ourselves to other people as a way to see how well we fit in. Anything that disrupts this process in even the smallest way can affect taken-for-granted assumptions that underlie social reality. It might help to think of this process as inserting grains of sand in an oyster to irritate it into creating a pearl of insight, or as a way to make systems of privilege itch, stir, and scratch and thereby reveal themselves for others to see. Or as planting seeds of doubt about the desirability and inevitability of the way things are and, by example, planting seeds of what might be.

Dare to make people feel uncomfortable, beginning with yourself. At the next local school board meeting, for example, you can ask why principals and other administrators are almost always white and male (unless your system is an exception that proves the rule), while the teachers they supervise and the lower-paid support staff are mostly women and people of color. Or look at the names and mascots used by local sports teams and see if they exploit the heritage and identity of Native Americans. If that's the case, ask principals and coaches and owners about it.[7] Consider asking similar kinds of questions about privilege and difference in your place of worship, workplace, and local government.

It may seem that such actions don't amount to much, until you stop for a moment and feel your resistance to doing them—worrying, for example, about how easily you could make people uncomfortable, including yourself. If you take that resistance to action as a measure of power, then your potential to make a difference is plain to see. The potential for people to feel uncomfortable is a measure of the power for change inherent in such simple acts of not going along with the status quo.

Some will say it isn't "nice" to make people uncomfortable, but systems of privilege do a lot more than make people feel uncomfortable, and there isn't anything "nice" about allowing that to continue. Besides, discomfort is an unavoidable part of any meaningful process of change. You can't grow without being willing to challenge your assumptions and take yourself to the edge of your competencies, where you're bound to feel uncomfortable. If you can't tolerate ambiguity, uncertainty, and discomfort, then you'll never get beneath superficial appearances or learn or change anything of much value, including yourself.

And if history is any guide, discomfort—to put it mildly—is also an unavoidable part of changing systems of privilege. As sociologist William Gamson noted in his study of social movements, "the meek don't make it."[8] To succeed, movements must be willing to disrupt business as usual and make those in power as uncomfortable as possible. Women didn't win the right to vote, for example, by reasoning with men and showing them the merits of their position. To even get men's attention, they had to take to the streets in large numbers at considerable risk to themselves. At the very least they had to be willing to suffer ridicule and ostracism, but it often got worse than that. In England, for example, suffragettes were jailed and, when they went on hunger strikes, were force fed through tubes run down their throats. The modern women's movement has had to depend no less on the willingness of women to put themselves on the line in order to make men so uncomfortable that they've had to pay attention and, eventually, to act.

It has been no different with the civil rights movement. Under the leadership of people like Martin Luther King, the movement was dedicated to the principle of nonviolence. As with the movement for women's suffrage, however, they could get white people's attention only through mass demonstrations and marches, to which whites typically responded with violence and intimidation.[9] As Douglas McAdam showed in his study of that period, the Federal government intervened and enacted civil rights legislation only when white violence against civil rights demonstrators became so extreme that the government was compelled to act.[10]

As the African American writer, orator, and abolitionist Frederick Douglass put it, "Power concedes nothing without a demand. It never has and it never will."[11] As much as anyone, I would like to believe Douglass is wrong, that all it takes to end an oppressive system of privilege is to point out the reality of oppression and the moral imperative that it not continue, and the receivers of privilege will somehow see the light and surrender their privilege without a fight. But history provides no reason to believe that to be true.

Openly choose and model alternative paths. As we identify paths of least resistance, we can identify alternatives and then follow them openly so that other people can see what we're doing. Paths of least resistance become more visible when people choose alternatives, just as rules become more visible when someone breaks them. Modeling new paths creates tension in a system, which moves toward resolution (like the irritated oyster). We don't have to convince anyone of anything. As Gandhi put it, the work begins with us trying to be the change we want to see happen in the world. If you think this has no effect, watch how people react to the slightest departures from established paths and how much effort they expend trying to ignore or explain away or challenge those who choose alternative paths.

Actively promote change in how systems are organized around privilege. The possibilities here are almost endless, because social life is complicated and privilege is everywhere. You can, for example,

Speak out for equality in the workplace.

Promote awareness and training around issues of privilege.

Support equal pay and promotion practices for everyone.

Oppose the devaluing of women, people of color, and people with disabilities, and the work they do, from dead-end jobs to glass ceilings.

Support the well-being of mothers, children, and people with disabilities, and defend their right to control their bodies and their lives.

Don't support businesses that are inaccessible to people with disabilities, and tell them why you don't.

Don't support businesses that engage in unfair labor practices, including union-busting. Support the formation of unions. Although the U.S. labor movement has a long history of racism, sexism, and ableism, unions are currently one of the few organized efforts dedicated to protecting workers from the excesses of capitalism.

Become aware of how class divisions operate in social systems, from workplaces to schools, and how this results in the oppression of blue- and white-collar workers. Find out, for example, if staff at your college or university are paid a living wage, and speak up if they aren't. There is a great silence in this country around issues of class, in part because the dominant cultural ideology presents the United States as a classless society. Break the silence.

Oppose the increasing concentration of wealth and power in the United States and the global economy. The lower, working, and lower-middle classes are the last to benefit from economic upturns and the first to suffer from economic downturns. Press politicians and candidates for public office to take a stand on issues of class, starting with the acknowledgment that they exist.

Object to the punitive dismantling of welfare and attempts to limit women's access to reproductive health services.

Speak out against violence and harassment wherever they occur, whether at home, at work, or on the street.

Support government and private services for women who are victimized by male violence. Volunteer at the local rape crisis center or battered-women's shelter. Join and support groups that intervene with and counsel violent men.

Call for and support clear and effective antiharassment policies in workplaces, unions, schools, professional associations, religious institutions, and political parties, as well as public spaces such as parks, sidewalks, and malls.

Object to theaters and video stores that carry violent pornography. This doesn't require a debate about censorship—just the exercise of freedom of speech to articulate pornography's role in the oppression of women and to express how its opponents feel about it.

Ask questions about how work, education, religion, and family are shaped by core values and principles that support privilege. You might accept women's entry into combat branches of the military or the upper reaches of corporate power as "progress," for example. But you could also raise questions about what happens to people and societies when political and economic institutions are organized around control, domination, "power over," and, by extension, competition and the use of violence. Is it progress to allow selected women to share control with men over oppressive systems?

Openly support people who step off the path of least resistance. When you witness someone else taking a risk—speaking out, calling attention to privilege and oppression—don't wait until later to tell them in private you're glad they did. Waiting until you're alone makes it safer for you but does the other person little good. Support is most needed when the risk is being taken, not later on, so don't wait. Make your support as visible and public as the courageous behavior that you're supporting.[12]

Support the right of women and men to love whomever they choose. Raise awareness of homophobia and heterosexism. For example, ask school officials and teachers about what's happening to gay and lesbian students in local schools. If they don't know, ask them to find out, since it's a safe bet these students are being harassed, suppressed, and oppressed by others at one of the most vulnerable stages of life. When sexual orientation is discussed, whether in the media or among friends, raise questions about its relation to male privilege. Remember that it isn't necessary to have answers to questions in order to ask them.

Pay attention to how different forms of oppression interact with one another. There has been a great deal of struggle within women's movements, for example, about the relationship between male privilege and privilege in other forms, especially those based on race, social class, and sexual orientation. White middle- and upper-middle-class heterosexual feminists have been criticized for pursuing their own agenda to the detriment of women who aren't privileged by class or race or sexual orientation. Raising concerns about glass ceilings that keep women out of top corporate and professional positions, for example, does little to help working- or lower-class women. There has also been debate over whether some forms of oppression are more important to attack first or produce more oppressive consequences than other forms.

One way out of this conflict is to realize that male privilege isn't problematic just because it emphasizes *male* dominance but because it values and promotes dominance and control as ends in themselves. In that sense, all forms of oppression draw support from common roots, and whatever we do that calls attention to those roots undermines *all* forms of privilege. If working against male privilege is seen simply as enabling some women to get a bigger piece of the pie, then some women probably will "succeed" at the expense of others who are disadvantaged by race, class, sexual orientation, and disability status. One could make the same argument about movements for racial justice. If it just means enabling well-placed people of color to get ahead, then it won't end racial oppression for the vast majority. But if we identify the core problem as *any* society organized around principles of domination and privilege, then changing *that* requires us to pay attention to all the forms of privilege those principles promote. Whether we begin with race or gender or disability or class or the capitalist system, if we name the problem correctly we'll wind up going in the same general direction.

Work with other people. This is one of the most important principles of participating in change. From expanding consciousness to taking risks, working with people who support what you're trying to do makes all the difference in the world. For starters, you can read and talk about books and issues and just plain hang out with other people who want to understand and do something about privilege and oppression. The roots of the modern women's movement were in consciousness-raising groups where women did little more than try to figure out how their lives were shaped by a patriarchal society. It may not have looked like much at the time, but it laid the foundation for huge social change.

One step down this path is to share a book like this one with someone and then talk about it. Or ask around about local groups and organizations that focus on issues of privilege. Attend a meeting and introduce yourself to the members. After reading a book or an article that you like, send an e-mail to the author or write in care of the publisher. It's easy to think authors don't want to be bothered by interested readers, but the truth is, they usually welcome it and respond. (I do!) Make contact. Connect to other people engaged in the same work. Do whatever reminds you that you're not alone in this.

It is especially important to form alliances across difference. What does this mean? As Paul Kivel argues, one of the keys to being a good ally is a willingness to listen—for whites to listen to people of color, for example—and to give credence to what people say about their own experience.[13] This isn't easy to do, of course, since members of dominant groups may not like what they hear about their privilege from those who are most damaged by it. It is difficult to hear anger and not take it personally, but that is what allies have to be willing to do. It's also difficult for members of privileged groups to realize how mistrusted they are by subordinate groups and to not take that personally as well. Kivel offers the following to give an idea of what people of color need from white allies (the same list could apply to allies across other forms of difference):

"respect"

"find out about us"

"don't take over"

"provide information"

"resources"

"money"

"take risks"

"don't take it personally"

"understanding"

"teach your children about racism"

"speak up"

"don't be scared of my anger"

"support"

"listen"

"don't make assumptions"

"stand by my side"

"don't assume you know what's best for me"

"put your body on the line"

"make mistakes"

"honesty"

"talk to other white people"

"interrupt jokes and comments"

"don't ask me to speak for my people"

One of the most important items on Kivel's list is for whites to talk to other white people. In many ways, the biggest challenge for members of privileged groups is to work with one another on issues of privilege rather than trying to help members of subordinate groups. Perhaps the biggest thing that men can do against sexism, for example, is to educate other men about patriarchy and confront other men about sexist behavior and the reality of male privilege. The same can be said about nondisabled people in relation to ableism and straights in relation to heterosexism. For members of privileged groups to become allies, they must recall Frederick Douglass's words, that "power concedes nothing without a demand" and add their weight to that demand. When dominant groups work against privilege, they do more than add their voices. They also make it more difficult for other members of dominant groups to dismiss calls for change as simply the actions of "special interest groups" trying to better their position.

Speaking out is, of course, a hard and risky thing to do, because receiving privilege depends on being accepted by other members of the privileged group. But it is not possible to both work to end privilege and hang on to it at the same time.

Don't keep it to yourself. A corollary of looking for company is not to restrict your focus to the tight little circle of your own life. It isn't enough to work out private solutions to social problems and keep them to yourself. It isn't enough to clean up your own act and then walk away, to find ways to avoid the worst consequences of privilege and oppression at home and inside you and think that's taking responsibility. Privilege and oppression aren't a personal problem that can be solved through personal solutions. At some point, taking responsibility means acting in a larger context, even if that means letting just one other person know what you're doing. It makes sense to start with yourself, but it's equally important not to end with yourself.

A good way to convert personal change into something larger is to join an organization dedicated to changing the systems that produce privilege and oppression. Most college and university campuses, for example, have student organizations that focus on issues of gender, race, sexual orientation, and disability. There are also national organizations working for change, often through local and statewide branches. Consider, for example, the National Organization for Women (NOW), the National Association for the Advancement of Colored People (NAACP), the National Conference for Community and Justice (formerly the National Conference of Christians and Jews), the National Gay and Lesbian Task Force, the Southern Poverty Law Center, the National Organization for Men Against Sexism, the Feminist Majority, the National Abortion Rights Action League, the Southern Christian Leadership Conference, the National Urban League, the American Association of Disabled Persons (AADP), Not Dead Yet, the American Council of the Blind, the National Association for the Deaf, ADAPT (American Disabled For Attendant Programs Today), and People First.

If all this sounds overwhelming, remember again that you don't have to deal with everything. You don't have to set yourself the impossible task of transforming society or even yourself. All you can do is what you can *manage* to do, secure in the knowledge that you're making it easier for other people—now and in the future—to see and do what *they* can do. So, rather than defeat yourself before you start, think small, humble, and doable rather than large, heroic, and impossible. Don't paralyze yourself with impossible expectations. It takes very little to make a difference. Small acts can have radical implications. As Edmund Burke said, if the main requirement for the perpetuation of evil is that good people do nothing, then the choice isn't between all or nothing, but between nothing and *something*.

Don't let other people set the standard for you. Start where you are and work from there. Make lists of all the things you could actually imagine *doing*—from reading another book about privilege to suggesting policy changes at school or work to protesting against capitalism to raising questions about who cleans the bathroom at home—and rank them from the most risky to the least. Start with the least risky and set reasonable goals ("What small risk for change will I take *today?*"). As you get more experienced at taking risks, you can move up your list. You can commit yourself to whatever the next steps are for you, the tolerable risks, the contributions that offer some way—however small it might seem—to help balance the scales. As long as you do something, it counts.

In the end, taking responsibility doesn't have to involve guilt and blame, letting someone off the hook, or being on the hook yourself. It simply means acknowledging an obligation to make a contribution to finding a way out of the trouble we're all in and to finding constructive ways to act on that obligation. You don't have to do anything dramatic or earth-shaking to help change happen. As powerful as systems of privilege are, they cannot stand the strain of lots of people doing something about it, beginning with the simplest act of naming the system out loud.

Acknowledgments

As this book goes to press, I'm mindful of people who have played an important part in the work that led to the writing of it. My thanks go to my sister, Annalee Johnson, who introduced me to training work around issues of privilege and encouraged me to take a chance. I'm especially grateful to my friend and colleague Jane Tuohy (to whom this book is dedicated) who more than anyone else has provided me with a vision of how I might use what I know in nonacademic settings, along with countless opportunities to do so. She has been a role model, a source of affirmation and support, and, at times, a worthy and thoughtful adversary in the heated discussions through which we continue to work through our understanding of these difficult issues as they play out in the real world of people's lives.

I'm also grateful to Shirley Harrell, Ed Hudner, Deat LaCour, Larry Mack, Robin Brown-Manning, and Helen Turnbull for all that I've learned in working with them, and to Leslie Brett, Kim Cromwell, Carolyn Gabel, and Anne Menard for how effectively they model lives dedicated to change. I'm especially grateful to my Race in America teaching partner, Fredrica Gray, for her strength and wisdom, her extraordinary breadth of knowledge, and her unfailing sense of humor when we've needed it most.

I give my thanks for the thoughtful feedback and suggestions offered by the several reviewers of the manuscript for the first edition including Leon F. Burrell, University of Vermont; Joan L. Griscom, William Paterson University; Betsy Lucal, Indiana University, South Bend; Tracy Ore, Saint Cloud State University; Fred L. Pincus, University of Maryland, Baltimore County; Sherwood Smith, University of Vermont; and Robert L. Walsh, University of Vermont. I'm especially thankful to Estelle Disch, University of Massachusetts, Boston; Paula Rothenberg, William Paterson University; and Michael Schwalbe, North Carolina State University, for challenging me in all the right places.

I am also indebted to reviewers and others who made valuable suggestions as I prepared the second edition. My thanks go to Joanne

Callahan, Kathy Castania (Cornell Migrant Program), Tracy Citeroni (University of Mary Washington), Jane Marantz Connor (Binghamton University), Monica D'Antonio (Rutgers University), Rachel David (Shoreline Community College), Ann Fischer (Southern Illinois University), Nicole Grant (Northern Kentucky University), Dr. Lori Handrahan (Oxford University), Andrea Herrera (University of Colorado–Colorado Springs), Brenda Hubbard (Central Washington University), Stuart Johnston (Luther College), Elizabeth Locke (Naropa University), Betty Garcia Mathewson (SUNY–Brockport), Ted McNeilsmith (Adams State College), Joan Morris (University of Central Florida), V. Spike Peterson (University of Arizona), Robert A. Principe (College of the Holy Cross), Dena Samuels (University of Colorado–Colorado Springs), Carole Sheffield (William Paterson University), Laura Szalacha (Brown University), Susan L. Thomas (Hollins University), Helen Turnbull (Human Facets, Inc.), Leah Ulansey (Maryland Institute College of Art), and Janice R. Welsch (Western Illinois University). I am especially grateful to Michael Schwalbe (North Carolina State University) and Marshall Mitchell (Washington State University) for their careful reading of the revised manuscript and, in addition, to Marshall for doing so much to open my eyes to nondisability privilege.

I also want to express my profound debt to the generations of activists, scholars, and writers whose courage and vision and hard work have given me the basis for most of what I know about these issues. Special thanks to Peggy McIntosh whose groundbreaking work did so much to clarify our understanding of the concept of privilege. And to those authors whose work I encountered so long ago that their insights have inadvertently slipped into my store of "common knowledge," I can offer only my appreciation and my apologies for being unable to give them proper attribution.

I would like to thank the wonderful editorial and production crew at Mayfield Publishing Company for their work on the first edition. For the second edition, I would like to thank my editor, Sherith Pankratz, for her abiding faith in this book and her continuing support for my work. My thanks also go to Editorial Assistant, Trish Starner and to the production team that expertly guided the manuscript into print—Mel Valentín, production editor; Tandra Jorgensen, production supervisor; and Preston Thomas, design manager.

My deepest gratitude is reserved for my comrade, soul mate, and partner in life, Nora L. Jamieson, for all that she does to nurture and challenge and support the writer in me, for all the moments when she has held the vision I'd lost sight of, and for the example of her own courage and wisdom in the face of a world in desperate need of both.

Notes

CHAPTER 1: RODNEY KING'S QUESTION

1. See Ellis Cose, *Rage of a Privileged Class* (New York: HarperPerennial, 1995).
2. For a fuller picture of what she's up against (and I'm not), see Joe R. Feagin and Melvin P. Sikes, *Living with Racism: The Black Middle Class Experience* (Boston: Beacon Press, 1994); and Ellis Cose, *Rage of a Privileged Class* (New York: HarperPerennial, 1995); and Joe R. Feagin and Karyn D. McKinney, *The Many Costs of Racism* (Lanham, MD: Rowman and Littlefield, 2003).
3. See, for example, Carol Brooks Gardner, *Passing By: Gender and Public Harassment* (Berkeley: University of California Press, 1995).

CHAPTER 2: PRIVILEGE, OPPRESSION, AND DIFFERENCE

1. "White, Male, and Worried," *BusinessWeek*, January 31, 1994, p. 55.
2. Personal correspondence, February 27, 2004.
3. Marilyn Loden and Judy B. Rosener, *Workforce America: Managing Employee Diversity as a Vital Resource* (Homewood, IL: Business One Irwin, 1991), p. 20.
4. See Michel Foucault, *History of Sexuality* (New York: Vintage, 1980); and M. Kay Martin and Barbara Voorhies, *Female of the Species* (New York: Columbia University Press, 1975); see also Anne Fausto-Sterling, "The Five Sexes: Why Male and Female Are Not Enough," *The Sciences* (March/April 1993), pp. 20–24.
5. The sections that follow are organized around types of behavior that are discussed in terms of racism by Joe R. Feagin and Melvin P. Sikes, *Living with Racism: The Black Middle-Class Experience* (Boston: Beacon Press, 1994), pp. 21–22. I apply them more broadly.
6. James Baldwin, "On Being 'White' . . . and Other Lies," *Essence*, 1984. Reprinted in David R. Roediger (ed.), *Black on White: Black Writers on What It Means to Be White*, pp. 177–80 (New York: Schocken Books, 1999).
7. For more on the social construction of whiteness, see Theodore W. Allen, *The Invention of the White Race*, vol. 1: *Racial Oppression and Social Control* (New York: Verso, 1994); vol. 2: *The Origin of Racial Oppression in Anglo-America* (New York: Verso, 1997); Charles Gallagher, "White Racial Formation: Into the Twenty-First Century," in Richard Delgado and Jean Stefancic (eds.), *Critical White Studies* (Philadelphia: Temple University Press, 1997), pp. 6–11; Christopher Wills, "The Skin We're In," in Delgado and Stefancic, pp. 12–14; Reginald Horsman, "Race and Manifest Destiny: The Origins of American Racial Anglo-Saxonism," in Delgado and Stefancic, pp. 139–44; and Kathleen Neal Cleaver, "The Antidemocratic Power of Whiteness," in Delgado and Stefancic, pp. 157–63.

8. Adrian Piper, "Passing for White, Passing for Black," in *Critical White Studies,* Richard Delgado and Jean Stefancic (eds.) (Philadelphia: Temple University Press, 1997), pp. 425–31.

9. Paul Kivel, *Uprooting Racism: How White People Can Work for Racial Justice,* rev. ed. (Gabriola Island, BC: New Society Publishers, 2002), p. 17.

10. For her now classic statement on the concept of privilege, see Peggy McIntosh, "White Privilege and Male Privilege: A Personal Account of Coming to See Correspondences Through Work in Women's Studies." Widely reprinted, it can be found in Anne Minas (ed.), *Gender Basics: Feminist Perspectives on Women and Men,* 2nd ed. (Belmont, CA: Wadsworth, 2000), pp. 30–38.

11. Ibid., p. 35.

12. Michell Fine and Adrienne Asch, "Disability beyond Stigma: Social Interaction, Discrimination, and Activism," in *Readings for Diversity and Social Justice,* Maurianne Adams, Warren J. Blumenfeld, Rosie Castañeda, Heather W. Hackman, Madeline L. Peters, and Ximena Zúñiga (eds.) (New York: Routledge, 2000), pp. 330–39.

13. Robert Terry, "The Negative Impact of White Values," in Benjamin P. Bowser and Raymond Hunt (eds.), *Impacts of Racism on White Americans* (Newbury Park, CA: Sage Publications, 1981), p. 120; see also Jean Baker Miller, who makes a similar observation in relation to gender in *Toward a New Psychology of Women,* 2nd ed. (Boston: Beacon Press, 1987).

14. Ellis Cose, *Rage of a Privileged Class* (New York: HarperCollins, 1993), p. 48.

15. Peggy McIntosh, "White Privilege and Male Privilege: A Personal Account of Coming to See Correspondences through Work in Women's Studies," in Anne Minas (ed.), *Gender Basics: Feminist Perspectives on Women and Men,* 2nd ed. (Belmont, CA: Wadsworth, 2000), pp. 30–38.

16. Much of what follows is drawn from Joseph Barndt, *Dismantling Racism: The Continuing Challenge to White America* (Minneapolis: Augsburg, 1991); Cose, *Rage of a Privileged Class;* Feagin and Sikes, *Living with Racism;* Paul Kivel, *Uprooting Racism: How White People Can Work for Racial Justice,* rev. ed. (Philadelphia: New Society Publishers, 2002); McIntosh, "White Privilege and Male Privilege"; and David T. Wellman, *Portraits of White Racism,* 2nd ed. (New York: Cambridge University Press, 1993).

17. U.S. Census Bureau, *Current Population Reports, Series P-60, Money Income in the United States, 2002* (Washington, D.C.: U.S. Government Printing Office, 2003); and *Statistical Abstract of the United States, 2002* (Washington, D.C.: U.S. Government Printing Office, 2003).

18. U.S. Census Bureau, *Current Population Reports, Series P-60, Money Income in the United States, 2002* (Washington, D.C.: U.S. Government Printing Office, 2003).

19. Brewster Thackeray, "State of the Union for People with Disabilities," National Organization on Disability (www.nod.org), 2003.

20. Kivel, *Uprooting Racism,* p. 122.

21. See Ruth Frankenberg, *The Social Construction of Whiteness: White Women, Race Matters* (Minneapolis: University of Minnesota Press, 1993).

22. Charlotte Bunch, "Not for Lesbians Only," *Quest* 11, no. 2 (Fall 1975).
23. Harry Brod, "Work Clothes and Leisure Suits: The Class Basis and Bias of the Men's Movement," in Michael Kimmel and Michael A. Messner (eds.), *Men's Lives* (New York: Macmillan, 1989), p. 280. Italics in original.
24. For a classic discussion of the meaning of oppression, see Marilyn Frye, *The Politics of Reality: Essays in Feminist Theory* (Trumansburg, NY: Crossing Press, 1983), pp. 1–16.

CHAPTER 3: CAPITALISM, CLASS, AND THE MATRIX OF DOMINATION

1. If you want to know more about this, two good basic sources are Richard C. Edwards, Michael Reich, and Thomas E. Weisskopf, *The Capitalist System*, 3rd ed. (Englewood Cliffs, NJ: Prentice Hall, 1986), and Joan Smith, *Social Issues and the Social Order: The Contradictions of Capitalism* (Cambridge, MA: Winthrop, 1981). See also Peter Saunders, *Capitalism* (Minneapolis: University of Minnesota Press, 1995). And for a more whimsical (but no less informative) view, try David Smith and Phil Evans, *Marx's "Kapital" for Beginners* (New York: Pantheon, 1982).
2. "House Passes Physician Bargaining Bill," Reuter's Online, June 30, 2000.
3. See Charles C. Ragin and Y. W. Bradshaw, "International Economic Dependence and Human Misery: 1938–1980: A Global Perspective," *Sociological Perspectives* 35(2), 1992, pp. 217–47. See also Harold R. Kerbo, *Social Stratification and Inequality*, 5th ed. (New York: McGraw-Hill, 2002), Chapter 14.
4. Joint Economic Committee, *The Concentration of Wealth in the United States* (Washington, D.C.: Joint Economic Committee of the U.S. Congress, 1986). See also Fred Brock, "The Richer Rich and Where They Live," *New York Times*, April 19, 1998; Barbara Crossette, "Worldwide, Most Are Consuming More, and the Rich Much More," *New York Times*, September 13, 1998; and David R. Francis, "Where Did All The Money Go? Not Far," *Christian Science Monitor*, July 16, 1997.
5. U.S. Census Bureau, *Current Population Reports*, Series P60-206, *Money Income in the United States, 1998* (Washington, D.C.: U.S. Government Printing Office, 1999), p. xiii.
6. For more on class, see Kerbo, *Social Stratification*, Chapters 6–9, and E. O. Wright, *Classes* (New York: Schocken, 1985).
7. See, for example, Leonard Beeghley, *Living Poorly in America: The Reality of Poverty and Pauperism* (New York: Praeger, 1983); Frances Fox Piven and Richard A. Cloward, *Regulating the Poor: The Functions of Public Welfare*, updated edition (New York: Vintage Books, 1993); and Jeffrey Reiman, *The Rich Get Richer and the Poor Get Prison: Ideology, Class, and Criminal Justice*, 7th ed. (New York: Macmillan, 2003).
8. See, for example, Martha R. Burt, *Over the Edge: The Growth of Homelessness in the 1980s* (New York: Russell Sage Foundation, 1992); and Peter H. Rossi,

Down and Out in America: The Origins of Homelessness (Chicago: University of Chicago Press, 1989).

9. For more on this, see Kerbo, *Social Stratification,* Chapter 11.

10. See Sheldon Danziger and Peter Gottschalk, *Uneven Tides: Rising Inequality in America* (New York: Russell Sage Foundation, 1993).

11. These figures come from General Social Survey data provided by the University of Chicago's National Opinion Research Center. James A. Davis and Tom W. Smith, *General Social Surveys, 1972–1996: Cumulative Code Book;* National Opinion Research Center data for 1998, taken from the Web site of the Institute for Social Research, University of Michigan, www.icpsr.umich.edu:8080/GSS/homepage.htm.

12. See, for example, Barbara Ehrenreich, *Fear of Falling: The Inner Life of the Middle Class* (New York: HarperCollins, 1989); and *Nickel and Dimed: On (Not) Getting By in America* (New York: Metropolitan Books, 2001); and Juliet B. Schor, *The Overworked American: The Unexpected Decline of Leisure* (New York: Basic Books, 1993).

13. Lester C. Thurow, *The Zero-Sum Society: Distribution and the Possibilities for Economic Change* (New York: Basic Books, 2001).

14. U.S. Census Bureau, *Negro Population: 1790–1915* (Washington, D.C.: U.S. Government Printing Office, 1918).

15. See Theodore W. Allen, *The Invention of the White Race,* vol. 1: *Racial Oppression and Social Control,* and vol. 2: *The Origin of Racial Oppression in Anglo-America* (New York: Verso, 1994, 1997).

16. For a vivid description and analysis of this, see W. E. B. Du Bois, *The Souls of Black Folk* (New York: Penguin, 1989), Chapter 8.

17. See Ronald Takaki, *Iron Cages: Race and Culture in 19th-Century America,* rev. ed. (New York: Oxford, 2000); and *Strangers from a Different Shore,* rev. ed. (Boston: Back Bay Books, 1998).

18. See the following by Immanuel Wallerstein: *The Modern World System* (New York: Academic Press, 1976); *The Capitalist World-Economy* (Cambridge: Cambridge University Press, 1979); *The Modern World System II: Mercantilism and the Consolidation of the European World Economy, 1600–1750* (New York: Academic Press, 1980); *The Modern World System III: The Second Era of Great Expansion of the Capitalist World-Economy, 1730–1840* (New York: Academic Press, 1989). See also Howard Zinn, *A People's History of the United States,* 20th anniv. ed. (New York: Perennial, 2003).

19. See Dee Brown, *Bury My Heart at Wounded Knee: An Indian History of the American West* (New York: Henry Holt, 1991).

20. See Allen, *Racial Oppression and Social Control* and *The Origin of Racial Oppression in Anglo-America,* Charles Gallagher, "White Racial Formation: Into the Twenty-First Century," in Richard Delgado and Jean Stefancic, eds., *Critical White Studies,* pp. 6–11 (Philadelphia: Temple University Press, 1997); Kathleen Neal Cleaver, "The Antidemocratic Power of Whiteness," in Delgado and Stefancic, pp. 157–63; Baldwin, "On Being 'White' . . . and Other Lies."

21. See Reginald Horsman, "Race and Manifest Destiny: The Origins of American Racial Anglo-Saxonism," in Delgado and Stefancic, pp. 139–44.

22. See David R. Roediger, *The Wages of Whiteness: Race and the Making of the American Working Class* (London and New York: Verso, 1991).

23. A powerful example of a situation in which this strategy ultimately failed is the great coal mine strike early in the twentieth century dramatized in the film *Matewan.*

24. Reich, Michael. "The Political-Economic Effects of Racism," in *The Capitalist System,* 3rd ed., Richard C. Edwards, Michael Reich, and Thomas E. Weisskopf (eds.) (Englewood Cliffs, NJ: Prentice Hall, 1986), pp. 304–11.

25. See Oliver Friedman, *"Review of Situation of Goodwill Industries in Connection with Fair Labor Standards Act"* (Goodwill Industries Int'l, Inc., Archives, 02/25/40).

26. See, for example, Heidi I. Hartmann, "The Family as the Locus of Gender, Class, and Political Struggle: The Example of Housework," *Signs: Journal of Women in Culture and Society* 6 (Spring 1981), pp. 366–94; Eli Zaretsky, *Capitalism, the Family, and Personal Life* (New York: Harper & Row, 1986); and Rosemary Tong, *Feminist Thought: A More Comprehensive Introduction* (Boulder, CO: Westview Press, 1998), Chapter 3.

27. See Barbara Reskin, "Bringing the Men Back In: Sex Differentiation and the Devaluation of Women's Work," *Gender and Society* 2, no. 1 (March 1988); and Irene Tinker, *Persistent Inequalities: Women and World Development* (New York: Oxford, 1990).

28. See Marilyn Waring, *If Women Counted: A New Feminist Economics* (San Francisco: HarperCollins, 1990).

29. See Patricia Hill Collins, *Black Feminist Thought: Knowledge, Consciousness, and the Politics of Empowerment,* 2nd ed. (New York: Routledge, 2000), Chapter 11; Estelle Disch, *Reconstructing Gender: A Multicultural Anthology,* 3rd ed. (New York: McGraw-Hill, 2002); p. 6. See also bell hooks, *Talking Back: Thinking Feminist, Thinking Black* (Boston: South End Press, 1989); Judith Lorber, *Paradoxes of Gender* (New Haven, CN: Yale University Press, 1995); Audre Lorde, *Sister Outsider: Essays and Speeches* (Freedom, CA: Crossing Press, 1984), especially pp. 114–23; and Gerda Lerner, "Reconceptualizing Differences Among Women," in Alison M. Jagger and Paula S. Rothenberg (eds.), *Feminist Frameworks,* 3rd ed. (New York: McGraw-Hill, 1993), pp. 237–48.

30. See Ronald Takaki, *Strangers from a Different Shore: A History of Asian-Americans,* p. 474.

31. See Kivel, *Uprooting Racism,* pp. 143–46.

CHAPTER 4: MAKING PRIVILEGE HAPPEN

1. See John F. Dovidio and Samuel L. Gaertner (eds.), *Prejudice, Discrimination, and Racism* (Orlando, FL: Academic Press, 1986).

2. The classic work on prejudice is Gordon W. Allport, *The Nature of Prejudice* (New York: Anchor Books, 1958). See also Dovidio and Gaertner, *Prejudice, Discrimination, and Racism,* and Daniela Gioseffi (ed.), *On Prejudice: A Global Perspective* (New York: Anchor Books, 1993).

3. There is a huge body of literature on the costs of privilege to women, homosexuals, and racial and ethnic minorities. See, for example, Joan Abramson, *Old Boys—New Women: Sexual Harassment in the Workplace* (New York: Praeger, 1993); American Association of University Women, *How Schools Shortchange Girls* (Washington, D.C.: American Association of University Women, 1992); Derrick Bell, *And We Are Not Saved: The Elusive Quest for Racial Justice* (New York: Basic Books, 1987); Derrick Bell, *Faces at the Bottom of the Well: The Permanence of Racism* (New York: Basic Books, 1992); Lois Benjamin, *The Black Elite: Facing the Color Line in the Twilight of the Twentieth Century* (Chicago: Nelson-Hall, 1991); Center for Research on Women, *Secrets in Public: Sexual Harassment in Our Schools* (Wellesley, MA: Wellesley College Center for Research on Women, 1993); Kim Chernin, *The Obsession: Reflections on the Tyranny of Slenderness* (New York: Harper & Row, 1981); David Gary Comstock, *Violence Against Lesbians and Gay Men* (New York: Columbia University Press, 1991); Cose, *Rage of a Privileged Class;* Angela Y. Davis, *Women, Race, and Class* (New York: Random House, 1981); Andrea Dworkin, *Woman Hating* (New York: Dutton, 1974); Barbara Ehrenreich and Deidre English, *For Her Own Good: 150 Years of Experts' Advice to Women* (New York: Anchor Books, 1978); Cynthia Fuchs Epstein, *Deceptive Distinctions: Sex, Gender, and the Social Order* (New Haven, CT: Yale University Press, 1990); Susan Faludi, *Backlash: The Undeclared War Against American Women* (New York: Crown, 1991); Feagin and Sikes, *Living with Racism;* Marilyn French, *Beyond Power: On Men, Women, and Morals* (New York: Summit Books, 1985); Marilyn French, *The War Against Women* (New York: Summit Books, 1992); Carol Brooks Gardner, *Passing By: Gender and Public Harassment* (Berkeley: University of California Press, 1995); Andrew Hacker, *Two Nations: Black and White, Separate, Hostile, Unequal* (New York: Scribner, 1992); Arlie Hochschild, *The Second Shift: Working Parents and the Revolution at Home* (New York: Viking/Penguin, 1989); bell hooks, *Ain't I a Woman: Black Women and Feminism* (Boston: South End Press, 1981); bell hooks, *Feminist Theory: From Margin to Center* (Boston: South End Press, 1984); bell hooks, *Talking Back;* bell hooks, *Sisters of the Yam: Black Women and Self-Recovery* (Boston: South End Press, 1993); Fran P. Hosken, *The Hosken Report: Genital and Sexual Mutilation of Females,* 4th rev. ed. (Lexington, MA: Women's International Network News, 1994); Kivel, *Uprooting Racism;* Laura Lederer (ed.), *Take Back the Night: Women on Pornography* (New York: Morrow, 1980); Lorber, *Paradoxes of Gender;* Lorde, *Sister Outsider;* Catharine A. MacKinnon, *Only Words* (Cambridge, MA: Harvard University Press, 1993); Brian McNaught, *Gay Issues in the Workplace* (New York: St. Martin's Press, 1993); Cherríe Moraga and Gloria Anzaldúa (eds.), *This Bridge Called My Back: Writings by Radical Women of Color,* 3rd ed. (New York: Third Woman Press, 2002); Michele A. Paludi, *Ivory Power: Sexual Harassment on Campus* (Albany: State University of New York Press, 1990); Suzanne Pharr, *Homophobia: A Weapon of Sexism* (Inverness, CA: Chardon Press, 1988); Adrienne Rich, *Of Woman Born* (New York: Norton, 1976); Diana E. H. Russell, *Sexual Exploitation: Rape, Child Sexual Abuse, and Workplace Harassment* (Beverly Hills, CA: Sage,

1984); Diana E. H. Russell (ed.), *Making Violence Sexy: Feminist Views on Pornography* (New York: Teachers College Press, 1993); Myra Sadker and David M. Sadker, *Failing at Fairness: How America's Schools Cheat Girls* (New York: Scribner, 1994); Peggy Reeves Sanday, *A Woman Scorned: Acquaintance Rape on Trial* (New York: Doubleday, 1996); Bernice Sandler, Lisa A. Silverberg, and Roberta M. Hall, *The Chilly Classroom Climate: A Guide to Improve the Education of Women* (Washington, D.C.: National Association for Women in Education, 1996); Marilyn Waring, *If Women Counted: A New Feminist Economics* (San Francisco: HarperCollins, 1990); Wellman, *Portraits of White Racism;* Cornel West, *Race Matters* (New York: Vintage, 1993); Naomi Wolf, *The Beauty Myth: How Images of Beauty Are Used Against Women* (New York: Morrow, 1991); James Woods and Jay H. Lucas, *The Corporate Closet: The Professional Lives of Gay Men in America* (New York: Free Press, 1993).

4. Feagin and Sikes, *Living with Racism*, pp. 15–17.

5. Walt Harrington, "On the Road with the President of Black America," *Washington Post Magazine,* January 25, 1987, p. W14.

6. See Douglas S. Massey and Nancy A. Denton, *American Apartheid: Segregation and the Making of the Underclass* (Cambridge, MA: Harvard University Press, 1998).

7. Claude M. Steele, "Race and the Schooling of Black Americans," *Atlantic Monthly,* April 1992, p. 73.

8. Benjamin, *Black Elite,* p. 20; Feagin and Sikes, *Living with Racism,* p. 25.

9. Marian Wright Edelman, *The Measure of Our Success: A Letter to My Children and Yours* (Boston: Beacon Press, 1992).

10. Quoted in Feagin and Sikes, *Living with Racism,* pp. 23–24.

11. See C. Bohmer and A. Parrot, *Sexual Assault on Campus* (New York: Lexington, 1993); A. Browne and K. R. Williams, "Gender Intimacy and Legal Violence: Trends From 1976 Through 1987," *Gender and Society* 7, no. 1(1993), pp. 78–98; Center for Research on Women, *Secrets in Public;* French, *War Against Women;* Allan G. Johnson, "On the Prevalence of Rape in the United States," *Signs: Journal of Women in Culture and Society* 6, no. 1(1980), pp. 136–46; Russell, *Sexual Exploitation.*

12. See Cose, *Rage,* pp. 31, 32–33; Feagin and Sikes, *Living with Racism,* p. 213.

13. R. Roosevelt Thomas, *Beyond Race and Gender: Unleashing the Power of Your Total Work Force by Managing Diversity* (New York: AMACOM, 1991), p. 102.

14. U.S. Bureau of the Census, *Statistical Abstract of the United States, 2001* (Washington, D.C.: U.S. Government Printing Office, 2002), Table 588.

15. Ibid., Tables 598 and 675.

16. Harris & Associates, "N.O.D./Harris Survey of Americans with Disabilities" (Washington, D.C.: National Organization on Disabilities, 2000).

17. Ibid.

18. Ibid., Table 666.

19. See Comstock, *Violence Against Lesbians and Gay Men;* McNaught, *Gay Issues in the Workplace;* Pharr, *Homophobia;* and Woods and Lucas, *The Corporate Closet.*

20. See Pharr, *Homophobia,* pp. 19, 23–24.

21. See Russell, *Sexual Exploitation;* Sanday, *A Woman Scorned.*

22. See Pharr, *Homophobia,* p. 26.

23. Much of this material is based on Joseph Barndt, *Dismantling Racism: The Continuing Challenge to White America* (Minneapolis: Augsburg, 1991), Chapter 3; and Kivel, *Uprooting Racism,* pp. 46–71.

24. See Ruth Frankenberg, *The Social Construction of Whiteness: White Women, Race Matters* (Minneapolis: University of Minnesota Press, 1993), pp. 60–61.

25. Barndt, *Dismantling Racism,* pp. 51–52; West, *Race Matters,* p. 19.

26. See Feagin and Sikes, *Living with Racism,* p. 53.

CHAPTER 5: THE TROUBLE WITH THE TROUBLE

1. For more on this, see Richard Delgado and Jean Stefancic, "Imposition," in Richard Delgado and Jean Stefancic (eds.), *Critical White Studies: Looking Behind the Mirror* (Philadelphia: Temple University Press, 1997), pp. 98–105.

2. R. Roosevelt Thomas, *Beyond Race and Gender: Unleashing the Power of Your Total Work Force by Managing Diversity* (New York: AMACOM, 1991), p. 41.

3. Marvin Harris, *Cows, Pigs, Wars, and Witches* (New York: Random House, 1974).

CHAPTER 6: WHAT IT ALL HAS TO DO WITH US

1. Kivel, *Uprooting Racism,* p. 91.

2. *Men Are from Mars . . .* is the title of a self-help book by John Gray, subtitled "A practical guide for improving communication and getting what you want in your relationships," published in 1992.

3. See David Thomas, "Racial Dynamics in Cross-Race Developmental Relationships," *Administrative Science Quarterly,* June 1993, pp. 169–94.

4. "Interview with Franklin McCain," in *The Eyes on the Prize Civil Rights Reader,* Clayborne Carson, David J. Garrow, Gerald Gill, Vincent Harding, and Darlene Clark Hine (eds.) (New York: Penguin, 1991), pp. 114–16.

CHAPTER 7: HOW SYSTEMS OF PRIVILEGE WORK

1. For more on patriarchy and how it works, see Allan G. Johnson, *The Gender Knot: Unraveling Our Patriarchal Legacy,* 2nd ed. (Philadelphia: Temple University Press, 2005). The general model for systems of privilege found there and in the present book derives from Marilyn French's monumental work on patriarchy, *Beyond Power: Men, Women, and Morals* (New York: Summit Books, 1985).

2. See, for example, Bernice Sandler et al., *The Chilly Classroom Climate: A Guide to Improve the Education of Women* (Washington, D.C.: National Association for Women in Education, 1996), part 4.

3. Quoted in ibid., p. 60.

4. Quoted in ibid., p. 62.

5. See Deborah Tannen, *You Just Don't Understand: Women and Men in Conversation* (New York: Morrow, 1990), and *Talking from 9 to 5* (New York: Morrow, 1994).
6. See, for example, Richard Butsch, "Class and Gender in Four Decades of Television Situation Comedy," *Critical Studies in Mass Communications* 9 (1992), pp. 387–99.
7. Feagin and Sikes, *Living with Racism*, p. 94.
8. Ibid., p. 229.
9. *America the Beautiful*, by Katharine Lee Bates, 1893.
10. For an excellent discussion of double binds, see Marilyn Frye, "Oppression," in *The Politics of Reality: Essays in Feminist Theory* (Trumansburg, NY: Crossing Press, 1983).
11. For more on how this works, see Arlie Hochschild, *The Second Shift: Working Parents and the Revolution at Home* (New York: Viking/Penguin, 2003).
12. See American Association of University Women, *How Schools Shortchange Girls* (Washington, D.C.: American Association of University Women, 1992); Feagin and Sikes, *Living with Racism;* Myra Sadker and David M. Sadker, *Failing at Fairness: How America's Schools Cheat Girls* (New York: Scribner, 1994); and Sandler et al., *The Chilly Classroom Climate.*
13. See American Association of University Women, *How Schools Shortchange Girls;* and Sadker and Sadker, *Failing at Fairness.*
14. See, for example, Beverly Daniel Tatum, *Why Are All the Black Kids Sitting Together in the Cafeteria?* 5th ed. (New York: Basic Books, 2003).
15. Wellman, *Portraits of White Racism.*
16. Jessie P. Guzman (ed.), *1952 Negro Yearbook* (New York: William H. Wise Co., 1952), pp. 275–79.
17. Wellman, *Portraits of White Racism*, p. 222.
18. Joel Kovel, *White Racism: A Psychohistory* (New York: Pantheon, 1970), p. 212.
19. See Alexander Thomas and Samuel Sillen, *The Theory and Application of Symbolic Interactionism* (Boston: Houghton-Mifflin, 1977).

CHAPTER 8: GETTING OFF THE HOOK

1. My sources for much of this chapter are Kivel, *Uprooting Racism*, pp. 50–62, and Wellman, *Portraits of White Racism*, pp. 207–209.
2. Christina Hoff Sommers, "The War Against Boys," *Atlantic Monthly,* May 2000, pp. 59–74.
3. Stanley Cohen, *States of Denial: Knowing About Atrocity and Suffering* (Cambridge, UK: Polity Press, 2001).
4. See William Ryan's classic book on this subject, *Blaming the Victim* (New York: Vintage, 1976).
5. See Douglas S. Massey and Nancy A. Denton, *American Apartheid: Segregation and the Making of the Underclass* (Cambridge, MA: Harvard University Press, 1998).

6. For a discussion of this, see Tatum, *Why Are All the Black Kids Sitting Together in the Cafeteria?*

7. Frankenberg, *Social Construction of Whiteness*, p. 49. Italics in original.

8. Edelman, *The Measure of Our Success.*

CHAPTER 9: WHAT CAN WE DO?

1. See Elizabeth Fisher, *Woman's Creation: Sexual Evolution and the Shaping of Society* (New York: McGraw-Hill, 1979); Gerda Lerner, *The Creation of Patriarchy* (New York: Oxford University Press, 1986).

2. This is what Warren Farrell means when he describes male power as mythical. In this case, he's right. See *The Myth of Male Power* (New York: Berkley Books, 1993).

3. J. R. Wilkie, "Changes in U.S. Men's Attitudes Towards the Family Provider Role, 1972–1989," *Gender and Society* 7, no. 2 (1993): 261–79.

4. The classic statement of how this happens is by Thomas S. Kuhn, *The Structure of Scientific Revolutions* (Chicago: University of Chicago Press, 1970).

5. Bonaro W. Overstreet, *Hands Laid Upon the Wind* (New York: Norton, 1955), p. 15.

6. My thanks to Joanne Callahan for suggesting the addition of this section.

7. For more on this, see Ward Churchill, "Crimes Against Humanity," *Z Magazine* 6 (March 1993), pp. 43–47. Reprinted in Margaret L. Andersen and Patricia Hill Collins (eds.), *Race, Class, and Gender,* 5th ed. (Belmont, CA: Wadsworth, 2004), pp. 439–46.

8. William A. Gamson, "Violence and Political Power: The Meek Don't Make It," *Psychology Today* 8 (July 1974), pp. 35–41.

9. For more on this, see the excellent PBS documentary of the civil rights movement, *Eyes on the Prize.*

10. Doug McAdam, *Political Process and the Development of Black Insurgency 1930–1970* (Chicago: University of Chicago Press, 1982).

11. Frederick Douglass, Speech Before the West Indian Emancipation Society (August 4, 1857), in *The Life and Writings of Frederick Douglass,* ed. Philip S. Foner, p. 437 (New York: International Publishers, 1950).

12. My thanks to Joanne Callahan for making me aware of this issue.

13. See Kivel, *Uprooting Racism*, part 3, "Being Allies."

Resources

PRIVILEGE AND OPPRESSION ACROSS TWO OR MORE DIMENSIONS

Adams, Maurianne, Warren J. Blumenfeld, Rosie Castañeda, Heather W. Hackman, Madeline L. Peters, and Ximena Zúñiga (eds.). *Readings for Diversity and Social Justice*. New York: Routledge, 2000.

Amott, Teresa L., and Julie A. Matthaei. *Race, Gender, and Work: A Multicultural Economic History of Women in the United States*. Rev. ed. Boston: South End Press, 1996.

Andersen, Margaret L., and Patricia Hill Collins (eds.). *Race, Class, and Gender: An Anthology*. 5th ed. Belmont, CA: Wadsworth, 2004.

Anzaldúa, Gloria (ed.). *Making Face, Making Soul/Haciendo Caras: Creative and Critical Perspectives by Feminists of Color*. San Francisco: Aunt Lute Books, 1990.

Belkhir, Jean G. *An Interdisciplinary Bibliography on the Intersection of Race, Class, and Gender*. Towson, MD: Institute for Teaching and Research on Women, Towson State University, 1996. This unique bibliography is regularly updated in an electronic edition at www.towson.edu/~vanfoss/rgc.htm.

Collins, Patricia Hill. *Black Feminist Thought: Knowledge, Consciousness, and the Politics of Empowerment*. 2nd ed. New York: Routledge, 2000.

Davis, Angela. *Women, Race, and Class*. New York: Random House, 1981.

Disch, Estelle. *Reconstructing Gender: A Multicultural Anthology*. 3rd ed. New York: McGraw-Hill, 2002.

Esty, Katharine, Richard Griffin, and Marcie Schorr Hirsch. *Workplace Diversity: A Manager's Guide to Solving Problems and Turning Diversity into a Competitive Advantage*. Holbrook, MA: Adams, 1995.

Gioseffi, Daniela, ed. *On Prejudice: A Global Perspective*. New York: Anchor Books, 1993.

Harro, Bobbie. "The Cycle of Liberation," in *Readings for Diversity and Social Justice*, Maurianne Adams, Warren J. Blumenfeld, Rosie Castañeda, Heather W. Hackman, Madeline L. Peters, and Ximena Zúñiga (eds.). New York: Routledge, 2000, pp. 463–469.

Higginbotham, Elizabeth. "Black Professional Women: Job Ceilings and Employment Sectors," in *Workplace/Women's Place*, Dana Dunn (ed.). Los Angeles: Roxbury, 1997, pp. 234–246.

hooks, bell. *Ain't I a Woman: Black Women and Feminism*. Boston: South End Press, 1981.

———. *Feminist Theory: From Margin to Center*. Boston: South End Press, 1984.

———. *Sisters of the Yam: Black Women and Self-Recovery*. Boston: South End Press, 1993.

———. *Talking Back: Thinking Feminism, Thinking Black*. Boston: South End Press, 1989.

Johnson, Allan G. *The Forest and the Trees: Sociology as Life, Practice, and Promise*. Philadelphia: Temple University Press, 1997.

Lerner, Gerda. "Reconceptualizing Differences Among Women," in *Feminist Frameworks,* 3rd ed., Alison M. Jaggar and Paula S. Rothenberg (eds.). New York, McGraw-Hill, 1993, pp. 237–248.

Loden, Marilyn, and Judy B. Rosener. *Workforce America: Managing Employee Diversity as a Vital Resource.* Homewood, IL: Business One Irwin, 1991.

Lorde, Audre. *Sister Outsider: Essays and Speeches.* Freedom, CA: Crossing Press, 1984.

Love, Barbara J. "Developing a Liberatory Consciousness," in *Readings for Diversity and Social Justice,* Maurianne Adams, Warren J. Blumenfeld, Rosie Castañeda, Heather W. Hackman, Madeline L. Peters, and Ximena Zúñiga (eds.). New York: Routledge, 2000, pp. 470–474.

McIntosh, Peggy. "White Privilege and Male Privilege: A Personal Account of Coming to See Correspondences Through Work in Women's Studies," in *Gender Basics: Feminist Perspectives on Women and Men,* 2nd ed. Anne Minas (ed.). Belmont, CA: Wadsworth, 2000. This classic article is widely reprinted in anthologies.

Mills, Nicholas, ed. *Debating Affirmative Action.* New York: Dell, 1994.

Moraga, Cherríe, and Gloria Anzaldúa (eds.). *This Bridge Called My Back: Writings by Radical Women of Color.* 3rd ed. New York: Third Woman Press, 2002.

Ore, Tracy E. *The Social Construction of Difference and Inequality: Race, Class, Gender, and Sexuality.* 2nd ed. New York: McGraw-Hill, 2002.

Roediger, David R. *The Wages of Whiteness: Race and the Making of the American Working Class.* New York: Verso, 1991.

Rosenblum, Karen E., and Toni-Michelle C. Travis (eds.). *The Meaning of Difference: American Constructions of Race, Sex and Gender, Social Class, and Sexual Orientation.* 3rd ed. New York: McGraw-Hill, 2003.

Rothenberg, Paula S. (ed.). *Race, Class, and Gender: An Integrated Study.* 6th ed. New York: St. Martin's, 2003.

———. *Invisible Privilege: A Memoir About Race, Class, and Gender.* Lawrence, KS: University Press of Kansas, 2000.

Ryan, William. *Blaming the Victim.* New York: Vintage, 1976.

St. Jean, Yanick, and Joe R. Feagin. *Double Burden: Black Women and Everyday Racism.* Armonk, NY: M. E. Sharpe, 1999.

U.S. Census Bureau. *Current Population Reports, Series P-60, Money Income in the United States.* Washington, D.C.: U.S. Government Printing Office. These reports are issued regularly with the latest data.

———. *Statistical Abstract of the United States.* Washington, D.C.: U.S. Government Printing Office. This volume is issued annually and is a readily available source of information on occupation, employment status, poverty, the distribution of wealth, educational attainment, etc.

Zinn, Howard. *A People's History of the United States.* New York: Perennial, 2003.

GENDER PRIVILEGE AND OPPRESSION

Abramson, Joan. *Old Boys—New Women: Sexual Harassment in the Workplace.* New York: Praeger, 1993.

American Association of University Women. *How Schools Shortchange Girls.* Washington, D.C.: American Association of University Women, 1992.

Andersen, Margaret L. *Thinking about Women: Sociological Perspectives on Sex and Gender.* 6th ed. New York: Macmillan, 2002.

Benokraitis, Nijole V. "Sex Discrimination in the 21st Century," in *Subtle Sexism: Current Practice and Prospects for Change,* Nijole V. Benokraitis (ed.). Thousand Oaks, CA: Sage, 1997, pp. 5–33.

———, and Joe R. Feagin. *Modern Sexism: Blatant, Subtle, and Covert Discrimination,* 2nd ed. Englewood Cliffs, N.J.: Prentice Hall, 1995.

Bohmer, Carol, and Andrea Parrot. *Sexual Assault on Campus.* New York: Lexington, 1993.

Brod, Harry. "Work Clothes and Leisure Suits: The Class Basis and Bias of the Men's Movement," in *Men's Lives,* Michael Kimmel and Michael A. Messner (eds.). New York: Macmillan, 1989, p. 289.

Browne, A., and K. R. Williams. "Gender Intimacy and Legal Violence: Trends From 1976 Through 1987." *Gender and Society* 7, no. 1(1993): 78–98.

Bunch, Charlotte. "Not for Lesbians Only." *Quest* 11, no. 2 (Fall 1975).

Center for Research on Women. *Secrets in Public: Sexual Harassment in Our Schools.* Wellesley, MA: Wellesley College Center for Research on Women, 1993.

Chernin, Kim. *The Obsession: Reflections on the Tyranny of Slenderness.* New York: Harper & Row, 1981.

Colwill, Nina L. "Women in Management: Power and Powerlessness," in *Workplace/Women's Place,* Dana Dunn (ed.). Los Angeles: Roxbury, 1997, pp. 186–197.

Corcoran-Nantes, Yvonne, and Ken Roberts. "'We've Got One of Those': The Peripheral Status of Women in Male-Dominated Industries," in *Workplace/Women's Place,* Dana Dunn (ed.). Los Angeles: Roxbury, 1997, pp. 271–287.

Dunn, Dana (ed.). *Workplace/Women's Place.* Los Angeles: Roxbury, 1997.

Dworkin, Andrea. *Woman Hating.* New York: Dutton, 1974.

Ehrenreich, Barbara, and Deidre English. *For Her Own Good: 150 Years of Experts' Advice to Women.* New York: Anchor Books/Doubleday, 1989.

———, and Arlie Russell Hochschild. *Global Woman.* New York: Owl Books, 2004.

Epstein, Cynthia Fuchs. *Deceptive Distinctions: Sex, Gender, and the Social Order.* New Haven, CT: Yale University Press, 1990.

Faludi, Susan. *Backlash: The Undeclared War Against American Women.* New York: Crown, 1991.

Fausto-Sterling, Anne. "The Five Sexes: Why Male and Female Are Not Enough." *Sciences* 33 (March/April 1993): 20–24.

———. *Myths of Gender: Biological Theories about Women and Men.* 2nd rev. ed. New York: Basic Books, 1992.

Federal Glass Ceiling Commission. *A Solid Investment: Making Full Use of the Nation's Human Capital.* Washington, D.C.: Federal Glass Ceiling Commission, 1995.

Fenstermaker, S., and C. West (eds.). *Doing Gender, Doing Difference: Inequality, Power, and Institutional Change.* New York: Routledge, 2002.

French, Marilyn. *Beyond Power: On Men, Women, and Morals.* New York: Summit Books, 1985.

———. *The War Against Women.* New York: Summit Books, 1992.

Frye, Marilyn. *The Politics of Reality: Essays in Feminist Theory.* Trumansburg, NY: Crossing Press, 1983.

Gardner, Carol Brooks. *Passing By: Gender and Public Harassment.* Berkeley: University of California Press, 1995.

Gilbert, Paula Ruth, and Kimberly K. Eby (eds.). *Violence and Gender: An Interdisciplinary Reader.* Englewood Cliffs, NJ: Prentice Hall, 2004.

Grewal, Inderpal, and Caren Kaplan (eds.). *Introduction to Women's Studies: Gender in a Transnational World.* New York: McGraw-Hill, 2001.

Haslett, Beth Bonniwell, and Susan Lipman. "Micro Inequities: Up Close and Personal," in *Subtle Sexism: Current Practice and Prospects for Change,* Nijole V. Benokraitis (ed.). Thousand Oaks, CA: Sage, 1997, pp. 34–53.

Helgesen, Sally. "Women's Ways of Leading," in *Workplace/Women's Place,* Dana Dunn (ed.). Los Angeles: Roxbury, 1997, pp. 181–185.

Hernandez, Daisy, Bushra Rehman, and Daisy Hernandez (eds.). *Colonize This!: Young Women of Color on Today's Feminism.* Seattle, WA: Seal Press, 2002.

Hochschild, Arlie. *The Second Shift: Working Parents and the Revolution at Home.* New York: Viking/Penguin, 2003.

Hosken, Fran P. *The Hosken Report: Genital and Sexual Mutilation of Females.* 4th rev. ed. Lexington, MA: Women's International Network News, 1994.

Jaggar, Alison M., and Paul Rothenberg (eds.). *Feminist Frameworks.* 3rd ed. New York: McGraw-Hill, 1993.

Johnson, Allan G. *The Gender Knot: Unraveling Our Patriarchal Legacy.* 2nd ed. Philadelphia: Temple University Press, 2005.

———. "On the Prevalence of Rape in the United States." *Signs: Journal of Women in Culture and Society* 6, no. 1(1980).

Jones, Ann. *Next Time She'll Be Dead: Battering and How to Stop It.* Boston: Beacon Press, 2000.

Kaufman, Michael, ed. *Beyond Patriarchy.* New York: Oxford, 1987.

Kerber, Linda K., and Jane Sherron De Hart (eds.). *Women's America: Refocusing the Past.* 6th ed. New York: Oxford University Press, 2003.

Kimmel, Michael. *Manhood in America: A Cultural History.* New York: Free Press, 1996.

———, R. W. Connell, and Jeff Hearn (eds.). *Handbook on Studies of Men and Masculinities.* Thousand Oaks, CA: Sage, 2004.

———, and Michael Messner (eds.). *Men's Lives.* 6th ed. Boston: Allyn & Bacon, 2003.

Lederer, Laura (ed.). *Take Back the Night: Women on Pornography.* New York: Morrow, 1980.

Loden, Marilyn. *Feminine Leadership.* New York: Random House, 1985.

Lorber, Judith. *Paradoxes of Gender.* New Haven, CT: Yale University Press, 1995.

MacKinnon, Catharine A. *Only Words.* Cambridge, MA: Harvard University Press, 1993.

Miller, Jean Baker. *Toward a New Psychology of Women.* 2nd ed. Boston: Beacon Press, 1987.

Minas, Anne (ed.). *Gender Basics: Feminist Perspectives on Women and Men.* 2nd ed. Belmont, CA: Wadsworth, 2000.

Moore, Lynda L. *Not As Far As You Think: The Realities of Working Women.* Lexington, MA: Lexington Books, 1986.

Morgan, Robin (ed.). *Sisterhood Is Global.* New York: Feminist Press, 1996.

Paludi, Michele A. *Sexual Harassment on College Campuses.* Albany: State University of New York Press, 1996.

Pharr, Suzanne. *Homophobia: A Weapon of Sexism,* expanded ed. Inverness, CA: Women's Project, 1997.

Reardon, Kathleen Kelley. "Dysfunctional Communication Patterns in the Workplace: Closing the Gap Between Women and Men," in *Workplace/Women's Place,* Dana Dunn (ed.). Los Angeles: Roxbury, 1997, pp. 165–180.

——. *They Don't Get It, Do They?* Boston: Little, Brown, 1995.

Rhode, Deborah L. *Speaking of Sex: The Denial of Gender Inequality.* Cambridge, MA: Harvard University Press, 1997.

Rich, Adrienne. *Of Woman Born.* New York: Norton, 1995.

Richardson, Laurel, Verta Taylor, and Nancy Whittier (eds.). *Feminist Frontiers.* 6th ed. New York: McGraw-Hill, 2003.

Rosenberg, Janet, Harry Perlstadt, and William R. F. Phillips. "'Now That We Are Here': Discrimination, Disparagement, and Harassment at Work and the Experience of Women Lawyers," in *Workplace/Women's Place,* Dana Dunn (ed.). Los Angeles: Roxbury, 1997, pp. 247–259.

Rotundo, Anthony. *American Manhood: Transformations in Masculinity from the Revolution to the Modern Era.* New York: Basic Books, 1993.

Russell, Diana E. H. *Sexual Exploitation: Rape, Child Sexual Abuse, and Workplace Harassment.* Beverly Hills, CA: Sage, 1984.

—— (ed.). *Making Violence Sexy: Feminist Views on Pornography.* New York: Teachers College Press, 1993.

——, and Roberta A. Harmes. *Femicide in Global Perspective.* New York: Teachers College Press, 2001.

Sadker, Myra, and David M. Sadker. *Failing at Fairness: How America's Schools Cheat Girls.* New York: Scribner, 1995.

Sanday, Peggy Reeves. *A Woman Scorned: Acquaintance Rape on Trial.* New York: Doubleday, 1996.

Sandler, Bernice, Lisa A. Silverberg, and Roberta M. Hall. *The Chilly Classroom Climate: A Guide to Improve the Education of Women.* Washington, D.C.: National Association for Women in Education, 1996.

Sapiro, Virginia. *Women in American Society: An Introduction to Women's Studies.* 5th ed. New York: McGraw-Hill, 2002.

Schultz, Vicki. "Reconceptualizing Sexual Harassment." *Yale Law Journal,* April 1998, pp. 1683–1805.

Stoltenberg, John. *Refusing to Be a Man.* New York: Meridian, 1989.

——. *The End of Manhood: A Book for Men of Conscience.* New York: Dutton, 1993.

Swerdlow, Marian. "Men's Accommodations to Women Entering a Nontraditional Occupation: A Case of Rapid Transit Operatives," in *Workplace/Women's Place*, Dana Dunn (ed.). Los Angeles: Roxbury, 1997, pp. 260–270.

Thorne, Barrie. *Gender Play: Girls and Boys in School.* New Brunswick, NJ: Rutgers University Press, 1993.

Waring, Marilyn. *If Women Counted: A New Feminist Economics.* San Francisco: HarperCollins, 1990.

Wilkie, J. R. "Changes in U.S. Men's Attitudes Towards the Family Provider Role, 1972–1989." *Gender and Society* 7, no. 2 (1993): 261–279.

Williams, Christine L. *Still a Man's World: Men Who Do Women's Work.* Berkeley: University of California Press, 1995.

Wolf, Naomi. *The Beauty Myth: How Images of Beauty Are Used Against Women.* New York: Morrow, 1991.

RACE PRIVILEGE AND OPPRESSION

Allen, Theodore W. *The Invention of the White Race: Racial Oppression and Social Control,* vols. 1–2. New York: Verso, 1994, 1997.

Allport, Gordon W. *The Nature of Prejudice.* New York: Anchor, 1958.

Baldwin, James. "On Being 'White'. . . and Other Lies." *Essence* 14 (April 1984): 90–92.

Barndt, Joseph. *Dismantling Racism: The Continuing Challenge to White America.* Minneapolis: Augsburg, 1991.

Barrett, James R., and David Roediger. "How White People Became White," in *Critical White Studies,* Richard Delgado and Jean Stefancic (eds.). Philadelphia: Temple University Press, 1997, pp. 402–406.

Bell, Derrick. *And We Are Not Saved: The Elusive Quest for Racial Justice.* New York: Basic Books, 1987.

———. *Faces at the Bottom of the Well: The Permanence of Racism.* New York: Basic Books, 1992.

Benjamin, Lois. *The Black Elite: Facing the Color Line in the Twilight of the Twentieth Century.* Chicago: Nelson-Hall, 1991.

Better, Shirley Jean. *Institutional Racism, A Primer on Theory and Strategies for Social Change.* Chicago: Burnham, 2002.

Bonilla-Silva, Eduardo. *Racism without Racists: Color-Blind Racism and the Persistence of Racial Inequality in the United States.* Lanham, MD: Rowman and Littlefield, 2003.

———. *White Supremacy and Racism in the Post–Civil Rights Era.* Boulder, CO: Lynne Rienner Publishers, 2001.

Carson, Clayborne, David J. Garrow, Gerald Gill, Vincent Harding, and Darlene Clark Hine (eds.). *The Eyes on the Prize Civil Rights Reader.* New York: Penguin, 1991.

Churchill, Ward. "Crimes Against Humanity." *Z Magazine* 6 (March 1993): 43–47. Reprinted in Margaret L. Andersen and Patricia Hill Collins (eds.). *Race, Class, and Gender,* 3rd ed. Belmont, CA: Wadsworth, 1998, pp. 413–420.

Collins, Patricia Hill. *Black Feminist Thought: Knowledge, Consciousness, and the Politics of Empowerment.* 2nd ed. New York: Routledge, 2000.

Correspondents of the *New York Times. How Race is Lived in America.* New York: Times Books, 2001.

Cose, Ellis. *The Rage of a Privileged Class.* New York: HarperCollins, 1993.

Davis, Angela Y. *Women, Race, and Class.* New York: Random House, 1981.

Delgado, Richard, and Jean Stefancic (eds.). *Critical White Studies.* Philadelphia: Temple University Press, 1997.

Doane, Ashley W., and Eduardo Bonilla-Silva (eds.). *White Out: The Continuing Significance of Racism.* New York: Routledge, 2003.

Dovidio, John F., and Samuel L. Gaertner (eds.). *Prejudice, Discrimination, and Racism.* Orlando, FL: Academic Press, 1986.

Du Bois, W. E. B. *The Souls of Black Folk.* New York: Penguin, 1996.

Edelman, Marian Wright. *The Measure of Our Success: A Letter to My Children and Yours.* Boston: Beacon Press, 1992.

Feagin, Joe R., and Karyn D. McKinney. *The Many Costs of Racism.* Lanham, MD: Rowman and Littlefield, 2003.

———, and Eileen O'Brien. *White Men on Race.* Boston: Beacon Press, 2003.

———, and Melvin P. Sikes. *Living with Racism: The Black Middle-Class Experience.* Boston: Beacon Press, 1995.

Frankenberg, Ruth. *The Social Construction of Whiteness: White Women, Race Matters.* Minneapolis: University of Minnesota Press, 1993.

Hacker, Andrew. *Two Nations: Black and White, Separate, Hostile, Unequal.* New York: Scribner, 1992.

Howard, Gary. *We Can't Teach What We Don't Know: White Teachers, Multiracial Schools.* New York: Teachers College Press, 1999.

Hurtado, Aida. *The Color of Privilege.* Ann Arbor: University of Michigan Press, 1999.

Kivel, Paul. *Uprooting Racism: How White People Can Work for Racial Justice.* Rev. ed. Philadelphia: New Society Publishers, 2002.

Kovel, Joel. *White Racism: A Psychohistory.* New York: Pantheon, 1970.

Lewis, Amanda. *Race in the Schoolyard.* Piscataway, NJ: Rutgers University Press, 2003.

Lipsitz, George. *The Possessive Investment in Whiteness: How White People Profit from Identity Politics.* Philadelphia: Temple University Press, 1998.

Marable, Manning, and Leith Mullings (eds.). *Let Nobody Turn Us Around: Voices of Resistance, Reform, and Renewal.* Lanham, MD: Rowman and Littlefield, 2000.

———. "Racism, Prisons, and the Future of Black America." Online at www.afsc.org/pwork/1200/122k05.htm.

Massey, Douglas S., and Nancy A. Denton. *American Apartheid: Segregation and the Making of the Underclass.* Cambridge, MA: Harvard University Press, 1998.

Piper, Adrian. "Passing for White, Passing for Black," in *Critical White Studies,* Richard Delgado and Jean Stefancic (eds.). Philadelphia: Temple University Press, 1997, pp. 425–431.

Rothenberg, Paula (ed.). *White Privilege: Essential Readings on the Other Side of Racism.* New York: Worth, 2002.

Shapiro, Thomas M. *The Hidden Cost of Being African-American: How Wealth Perpetuates Inequality.* New York: Oxford University Press, 2003.

Steele, Claude M. "Race and the Schooling of Black Americans." *Atlantic Monthly,* April 1992, p. 73.

Takaki, Ronald. *Strangers from a Different Shore: A History of Asian-Americans.* Rev. ed. Boston: Back Bay Books, 1998.

Tatum, Beverly Daniel. *Why Are All the Black Kids Sitting Together in the Cafeteria?* 5th ed. New York: Basic Books, 2003.

Terry, Robert. "The Negative Impact on White Values," in *Impacts of Racism on White Americans,* Benjamin P. Bowser and Raymond Hunt (eds.) Newbury Park, CA: Sage, 1981.

Thomas, Alexander, and Samuel Sillen. *Racism and Psychiatry.* New York: Brunner/Mazel, 1972.

Thomas, David. "Racial Dynamics in Cross-Race Developmental Relationships." *Administrative Science Quarterly* (June 1993): 169–194.

Thomas, Roosevelt R. *Beyond Race and Gender: Unleashing the Power of Your Total Work Force by Managing Diversity.* New York: AMACOM, 1991.

Van Ausdale, Debra, and Joe R. Feagin. *The First R: How Children Learn Race and Racism.* Lanham, MD: Rowman and Littlefield, 2002.

Wellman, David T. *Portraits of White Racism.* 2nd ed. New York: Cambridge University Press, 1993.

West, Cornel. *Race Matters.* New York: Vintage, 1993.

Western Prison Project. "The Prison Index." Online at www.westernprison project.org/Publications/Factsheets/Prison_Index_Incarceration_Fact_ Sheet.pdf.

PRIVILEGE, OPPRESSION, AND SEXUAL ORIENTATION

Abelove, Henry, Michele Aina Barale, and David M. Halperin (eds.). *The Lesbian and Gay Studies Reader.* New York: Routledge, 1993.

Baker, Dan, and Sean Strub. *Cracking the Corporate Closet.* New York: HarperCollins, 1993.

Blumenfeld, Warren. *Homophobia: How We All Pay the Price.* Boston: Beacon Press, 1992.

Comstock, David Gary. *Violence Against Lesbians and Gay Men.* New York: Columbia University Press, 1991.

Gross, Larry P., and James D. Woods (eds.). *The Columbia Reader on Gays and Lesbians in Politics, Society, and the Media.* New York: Columbia University Press, 1999.

McNaught, Brian. *Gay Issues in the Workplace.* New York: St. Martin's, 1993.

Miller, Neil. *Out of the Past: Gay and Lesbian History from 1869 to the Present.* New York: Vintage, 1995.

Pharr, Suzanne. *Homophobia: A Weapon of Sexism.* Expanded ed. Inverness, CA: Women's Project, 1997.

Warner, Michael. *The Trouble with Normal.* Cambridge, MA: Harvard University Press, 2000.

Woods, James, and Jay H. Lucas. *The Corporate Closet: The Professional Lives of Gay Men in America.* New York: Free Press, 1993.

SOCIAL CLASS PRIVILEGE AND OPPRESSION

Aronowitz, Stanley. *How Class Works: Power and Social Movement.* New Haven, CT: Yale University Press, 2003.

Danziger, Sheldon, and Peter Gottschalk. *Uneven Tides: Rising Inequality in America.* New York: Russell Sage Foundation, 1993.

Domhoff, G. William. *Who Rules America? Power and Politics.* 4th ed. New York: McGraw-Hill, 2001.

Ehrenreich, Barbara. *Fear of Falling: The Inner Life of the Middle Class.* New York: HarperCollins, 1990.

———. *Nickel and Dimed: On (Not) Getting By in America.* New York: Metropolitan Books, 2001.

Gilbert, Dennis. *The American Class Structure in an Age of Growing Inequality.* 6th ed. Belmont, CA: Wadsworth, 2002.

Halpern, Greg. *Harvard Works Because We Do.* New York: W. W. Norton, 2003.

hooks, bell. *Where We Stand: Class Matters.* New York: Routledge, 2000.

Kerbo, Harold R. *Social Stratification and Inequality.* 5th ed. New York: McGraw-Hill, 2002.

Neubeck, Kenneth J., and Noel A. Cazenave. *Welfare Racism: Playing the Race Card Against America's Poor.* New York: Routledge, 2001.

Reiman, Jeffrey. *The Rich Get Richer and the Poor Get Prison: Ideology, Class, and Criminal Justice.* 7th ed. Upper Saddle River, NJ: Pearson Allyn & Bacon, 2003.

Schor, Juliet B. *The Overworked American: The Unexpected Decline of Leisure.* New York: Basic Books, 1993.

Sennett, Richard, and Jonathan Cobb. *The Hidden Injuries of Class.* New York: W. W. Norton, 1993.

Shipler, David K. *The Working Poor: Invisible in America.* New York: Knopf, 2004.

DISABILITY STATUS PRIVILEGE AND OPPRESSION

Charlton, James I. *Nothing About Us Without Us: Disability Oppression and Empowerment.* Berkeley: University of California Press, 2000.

Condeluci, A. *Interdependence: The Route to Community.* 2nd ed. New York: St. Lucie Press, 1995.

Davis, Lennard J. *The Disability Studies Reader.* New York: Routledge, 1997.

Fine, Michelle, and Adrienne Asch. "Disability beyond Stigma: Social Interaction, Discrimination, and Activism," in *Readings for Diversity and Social Justice,* Maurianne Adams, Warren J. Blumenfeld, Rosie Castañeda, Heather W. Hackman, Madeline L. Peters, and Ximena Zúñiga (eds.). New York: Routledge, 2000, pp. 330–339.

Johnson, Mary. *Make Them Go Away: Clint Eastwood, Christopher Reeve and the Case Against Disability Rights.* The Advocado Press, 2003.

Lane, Harlan L. *The Mask of Benevolence: Disabling the Deaf Community.* Chicago: Independent Publishers Group, 2000.

National Women's Studies Association Journal 14, no. 3 (Fall, 2002), issue devoted to Feminist Disability Studies.

Shapiro, Joseph. *No Pity.* New York: Three Rivers Press, 1993.

Smith, Bonnie, and Beth Hutchinson (eds.). *Gendering Disability.* Piscataway, NJ: Rutgers University Press, 2004.

Wendell, Susan. *The Rejected Body: Feminist Philosophical Reflections on Disability.* New York: Routledge, 1996.

Credits

Index